Best wishes
to
my dear friend
Linda

from
Lillian Jones Dowling

One of the Boys but Always a Lady

The author at the time of the book's action—1942 to 1947.

One of the Boys but Always a Lady

The Life of a Red Cross Recreation Worker in Combat Troop Camps in Australia during the War with Japan

Lillian Jones Dowling

VANTAGE PRESS
New York

WALTZING MATILDA. Music by Marie Cowan, words by A.B. Paterson.
Copyright © 1936, 1941 by Carl Fischer, Inc.
Used by permission.

FIRST EDITION

All rights reserved, including the right of
reproduction in whole or in part in any form.

Copyright © 1998 by Lillian Jones Dowling

Published by Vantage Press, Inc.
516 West 34th Street, New York, New York 10001

Manufactured in the United States of America
ISBN: 0-533-12238-4

Library of Congress Catalog Card No.: 96-90990

0 9 8 7 6 5 4 3 2 1

To the honored memory of those who
fought and died for our country—for us

Contents

Acknowledgments ix
Preface xi

I. They Were Heroes 1
II. Jonesie Goes to Washington 2
III. Assigned to the Land Down Under 9
IV. Crossing the Pacific Pacific 12
V. Getting Introduced to a Strange New Country 15
VI. A Love Affair with Thousands 21
VII. Sights and Sounds of Sydney 62
VIII. Eagles and Airplanes Both Have Wings 66
IX. Adelaide River—Bear Every Hardship, Cope with Every Inconvenience, Graciously, and Don't Complain 69
X. Ssh! Ssh! It's All a Big Secret! 87
XI. Toowoomba, Good Place to Sit Down 112
XII. Happy Boredom aboard a Homeward-Bound Troopship 139
XIII. Holding Hands with the Sick in San Francisco 141
XIV. Just As Though Nothing Had Ever Happened 151

Historical Reference:
A Brief Account of the War in the Pacific 153

Acknowledgments

I owe an inestimable debt of gratitude to my great and good friend Marlene Mitchell, whose computer expertise and wise counsel have enabled me to put this personal story of events in the Pacific theater of World War II onto the printed page, and to my dear partner, Edwin Martinson, for his encouragement throughout this project.

Preface

This is a story of the human side of World War II, the war in the Pacific, the war against Japan. It is an account of my three years as a Red Cross Recreation Worker with combat troops on their camps in Australia: seven months with the Marine Corps, six with the Army; seven with a Navy Construction Battalion, and seven in a Navy R & R (Rest and Recreation) center for submariners, along with preparations for and layovers between assignments. The latter part of the book tells briefly of my two years that followed as a Red Cross Recreation Worker in an Army evacuation hospital in San Francisco.

Though much of this story is unbelievable, every word is true.

Some who read my book may say they have read a vignette of history, some might say they have read a joke book; some might say they have read a book of weird incredible but true happenings; some that they have read a tragic multiple love story; others that they learned how to become a dinky di Aussie. In fact, it is all of these, but one observation was the same for all who have read the manuscript: they all said they were there with me, giving care and comfort to those who laid their lives on the line for us.

When you pick up this book, be ready to walk into a world totally different from the relaxed, calm, contented peacetime one in which you are living today. In war, a feeling of extreme urgency pervades the atmosphere, an air of tension is everywhere. Everything is on an emergency basis. Feelings are intense; friendships are immediate and intense; love affairs are immediate and intense as well. Humor is often bawdy. The soft-spoken, whimsically humorous nuances of front parlor pleasantry are now too blandly milquetoast to fit the scene. Language is often coarse. And everything, everything, is temporary. Grasp the moment while you can. Tomorrow? Well, tomorrow you may be dead. Yes, tomorrow you may be dead, and this strong probability dominates your entire psyche. To face it, one needs all the courage he can muster.

I have placed at the end of the book a brief history of the war with Japan. You may not even glance at it. Or you may refer to it to clarify in your mind some particular portion of the war. People who have read it through say they have gained an understanding and knowledge of its events in their sequence, and most of them have said that for the first time they now understand the war as a whole.

As we read the book, I feel it is well for us to remember the words of Benjamin Franklin as he left the hall in Philadelphia at the end of the Constitutional Convention in 1787. A passerby asked, "What kind of a government did you give us, Mr. Franklin?" He replied, "A DEMOCRACY. IF YOU CAN KEEP IT."

One of the Boys but Always a Lady

I
They Were Heroes

Here it is, fifty years later, and I still cry when I think of them, those heroic combat troops I lived and worked with in Australia during World War II. They were heroes, all of them. It surely takes heroism to look death in the face and know that you are most likely going to die but still go ahead without batting an eye. And they did die, nearly all of them, as they knew they would, and still they went ahead. There is a strange thing about heroism: the least likely of them all, the very least promising, the one you wonder why he's in the service at all, may be the very one who rises to the greatest heights of self-sacrifice and unbelievable acts of physical strength and endurance, willingly giving his life for his country and his comrades. I learned, very early, one of my first and best lessons of the war: never count anybody out. I learned also to overlook some minor character frailties in favor of the greater good in these and, therefore, in all people.

II
Jonesie Goes to Washington

It was "The Good War," as it has now been called. The issues were clear-cut. We were fighting, good versus evil, in Europe, fighting Hitler and his Nazism, with which he had infected whole populations on the continent, and we were fighting for the very survival of our own nation in the face of the incredible arrogance of the Japanese in thinking they could take possession of the United States. It was a war in which we lost half of our Navy, a third of our merchant shipping, four hundred thousand lives, and immense resources. Winston Churchill was spending $86 million a day in the European theater and already many of our troops were ashore in Europe, but the galvanizing impact for the United States came with the Japanese bombing of Pearl Harbor on the island of Oahu in Hawaii, December 7, 1941.

The emotional climate of the entire country changed overnight. The war, up to that moment, was far away and did not absolutely, directly, concern each and every United States citizen, but now our very nation was attacked. Immediately a deep fog of gloom descended on our entire populace, and every person in our whole country was consumed by a burning desire to do all he or she could to assist in the war effort.

At the time, I was a business teacher at South Division High School in Milwaukee, Wisconsin, and in my typewriting classes never was this old chestnut more apropos: "Now is the time for all good men to come to the aid of their country."

I remember, as though it were yesterday, my weekend trip home to my family on our farm near Wautoma, Wisconsin, forty miles west of Oshkosh. It was the end of February 1942. The only topic of conversation was what we, as a family, could do to help. Not only had our fleet been immobilized at Pearl Harbor with the sinking of all the ships anchored there, four thousand lives and 250 military planes lost, but the Japanese had immediately taken our other Pacific island possessions: Wake, Guam, and the Philippine Islands. Before Pearl Harbor, the Japanese ruling military clique had led their army in an aggressive takeover of about one-third of China with cruel atrocities and also all of French Indochina. And now they had seized Hong Kong, the whole Malay Peninsula, and Singapore. There was now widespread apprehension lest the Japanese attack our own continental United States. A dark purple pall hung over everyone everywhere.

We decided among us that we could make two contributions to the war effort: farm production and the direct services of one member of the family. Among our seven siblings, I was the only one young enough, old enough, and unencumbered enough, to go into war work.

Consequently, in the ensuing weeks I took a Civil Service examination in office procedures which led to my being granted an office position in the war effort in Washington, D.C. My school board graciously granted me a leave of absence for the duration. They spoke of their desire to do what they, too, could to help the war effort, and although they could not pay me a salary, they did grant me teaching credit toward my pension for the time I was away. The time away turned out to be five years, and this deed on their part has been one for which I have never ceased to be grateful.

June twentieth found me in Washington in the Typing Pool of the Board of Economic Warfare, located in one of the enormous Quonset huts which had been set up along Pennsylvania Avenue.

What was inside that Quonset hut turned out to be a disappointment. I was placed at the lowest level of the Civil Service scale, clearly overqualified, and soon was appointed Manager of the Typing Pool. The level of skill among typists there was so low that my students finishing their first semester of typing could have done better. Not only were these typists' manual skills grossly deficient, but their level of general education was horrifyingly lower yet. One example still stands out in my mind: A shipment of special camera lenses en route to our forces in Europe for photographing the European mainland and labeled to be urgently expedited went around the world five times before anyone discovered that "Nfd." stood for Newfoundland. Incredible! I immediately started an in-service training program in place geography. Other innovations continued and still I was on the lowest rung of the salary scale, making barely a subsistence wage. A friend in the government suggested that I return home and make a Civil Service application at a higher level. Although this was an option, I scouted around Washington for other lines of war work.

I was turned down by the Army when some high-ranking officers interviewed me and asked what organizations I belonged to and I mentioned that I was a member of the American Federation of Teachers, the national teachers' labor union. I can still see them rolling their eyes as they told me, "Don't call us; we'll call you."

These job hunting excursions continued during my lunch hour, and one day I walked into the "Marble Palace," which is what people called the rather small, exquisitely beautiful building that housed the national headquarters of the American Red Cross. I was immediately ushered into the presence of a tall, austere middle-aged woman who told me they were accepting recruits for overseas duty. Did I think I could handle a job as a recreation worker?

Having spent thousands of unpaid extracurricular hours on similar activities for students at my high school, I responded, "Yes, I think I can."

"Where would you like to be sent?"

"As close to the fighting as they will allow a petticoat."

In ten minutes I was hired as a recreation worker for able-bodied combat troops in their camps. I had ten days to close all my affairs in the States and report back to her office with, except for uniforms, everything I would need to survive two years in backcountry under the most primitive conditions. All of my belongings, including uniforms, were to fit into a small boxlike trunk called a footlocker. It is called a footlocker because it stands at the foot of an Army cot and was, and probably still is, standard issue to servicepeople.

Although subletting my apartment and storing all my possessions was a challenge, it could not compare with this last requirement. What does one provide oneself for a two-year survival in the wild, condensed into a footlocker? I took a comb, hairbrush, bobby pins, hair pins, a little face powder, rouge and lipstick for special occasions, two toothbrushes, two tubes of toothpaste, three sets of undies, and—what to do about Kotex? Kotex for two years would have filled more than a footlocker, and for days I was absolutely stumped. At last I bought six cotton diapers, which stowed away nicely and proved a serendipitous choice. I still keep one as a secret souvenir.

Back in Washington, reporting to my cold, dour recruiting officer at the Marble Palace, I told her I would like to bring some extra recreational materials which would have to be accommodated outside of the footlocker. She rose from her chair, stood bolt upright, and pronounced in icy, stentorial tones, "MOST IRREGULAR!"

As time went on and I reported to her dutifully once a week, I was MOST IRREGULAR time after time, and I often wondered if she would keep me on in spite of my gross irregularities, but they became fewer as I became more and more immersed in the rigidly structured life of the American Red Cross, and we even began to feel some affection for each other.

The plan was for the overseas workers to be given a two-week indoctrination course and then to be transported to our overseas assignments, the location of which was not to be made known to us until departure. However, passenger space on ships was in such extremely short supply that it was five months before I was told I was going to Australia and I must be ready to leave in a half hour. As a matter of fact, I lived for five months on a one-half-hour alert, and that in itself was one of the major stresses of my wartime life. A challenging problem for the Red Cross and, particularly, for my recruiting officer was what to do with us while we awaited transport. At first they settled on the idea of repeating the two-week indoctrination course. Would you believe that five times I spent two weeks of eight-hour days learning the tightly structured Red Cross "Channels," plus the four cardinal characteristics and duties of Red Cross overseas workers? Those duties are so deeply etched in my consciousness that even now I follow them as by reflex action. When I die, I know the autopsy will show the four precepts burned into the bone of my forehead: MEET THE NEED. (This was the cardinal precept and it was repeated as seemingly every other sentence for all those ten weeks of 8-hour days, which added up to 400 hours.) The other three, which were dwelt upon with all appropriate might and main, were: Absolute Confidentiality; Bear Every Hardship, Cope with Every Inconvenience, Graciously, and Don't Complain; and Don't Ask Prying Questions about the Military. To this day, people can tell me earth-shattering confidences and I will not repeat one syllable, and a sense of things that are none of my business warns me away from personal inquisitiveness. When it comes to bearing hardships and coping with inconveniences graciously and not complaining, I can't even bring myself to mention to a waitress that there is a hair in my soup. Once, while I was incapacitated in a hospital, I was instructed to report as to when daily increasing doses of a dangerous drug became unbearable. After some time, three doctors and two nurses appeared and said that the next day's increase would bring me to a lethal dose of the medication, but I still could not bring myself to complain. As for MEET THE NEED, I have become a patsy for every charitable organization in this whole country.

After taking me through the two-week indoctrination course five times, even they decided enough is enough, and they scratched their heads for interim fill-in assignments.

I was sent for a two-week tour of duty helping run the recreation activities at the Army post Fort Belvoir in Virginia. The lady who ran the operation was the widow of a World War I Master Sergeant who had come home from the terrible dangers and rigors of service on the front lines in France, only to be shot and killed in an outdoor toilet on the post by a renegade Army marksman.

My daily journey to this assignment involved a long bus trip which led me from the racially tolerant District of Columbia into the highly intolerant State of Virginia. When we entered the State of Virginia the driver pulled the bus to the side of the road and announced, "All whites to the front of the bus. All blacks to the back of the bus." This requirement ended in the 1960s, but at the time I was shocked to find this attitude would exist even in the 1940s. I refused to move to the front because I was engaged in a pleasant conversation with a black seatmate toward the rear of the bus. At this point the driver became authoritative and sternly ordered, "Lady, the bus will not move until you sit in the front." So I came to the front, stood, and made a speech. "A regulation like this is unconscionable and this practice will end, and I shall work hard to bring it to its end. I urge that all of you do so, too." Too bad it took another twenty years to reach this goal!

My recruiting officer, with whom I was becoming less and less IRREGULAR, came up with another idea for an assignment while awaiting transport. I was to help the manager of the local YWCA with her office work, and I dutifully got her caught up on her back correspondence, which had been accumulating for months due to lack of available secretarial help.

Now the situation called for an even more imaginative assignment, and I was sent to work in a Jewish community center in New York City. This proved to be fascinating, and I learned a great deal about ecumenism, loving kindness, and New York City life. I was a girl of many duties, from office, to kitchen, to recreation hall.

By this time the weeks had rolled on and it was now Hanukkah time. I helped with a large Hanukkah party attended by several hundred participants. At this party I was startled and filled with curiosity about what various people were doing. One person would come up to another and whisper in the other's ear. This was followed by the most heart-wrenching sigh of horror and accompanying words of distress before rejoining the party. Finally, I could no longer bear the suspense and I asked one of them if she would mind telling me what the conversation was about inasmuch as it was pervasive through the whole group. She said, barely able to hold back the tears, "We just heard that Hitler has now killed a million Jews. We do not know where it will end, and we feel helpless in the face of it. We can hardly bear it." That was only toward the end of 1942, and the world knows that Hitler and his fellow Nazis continued the Holocaust activities until May of 1945, two and one-half years and 5 million Jews later. Even now, if one were to ask any Jewish friend or acquaintance about his or her family, one would be sure to hear about some close relative sacrificed to this horror.

The Hanukkah party continued, but one could see that everyone there was struggling to keep a party spirit. I have often wondered if I would have been able to handle any direct knowledge of the Holocaust had I been sent to the European theater. A friend who went through the Red Cross indoctrination course with me and who was assigned to Europe visited Dachau the day after the liberation. She lost her mind.

Life in Washington while awaiting assignment was very different from daily domestic living. We were housed in respectable but far from fancy hotels. Many of us, including me, lived at the Harrington

Hotel as pleasantly as one could live on a one-half-hour transportation alert. We were allowed to go anywhere we wanted so long as we let the hotel employees know where we could be reached immediately and exactly what time we would return. The rooms were comfortable and the food was quite acceptable, prepared in a southern cooking style. The hotel, however, was plagued, as I am sure all others were, with cockroaches, which as we know are the bane of every southerner's existence. They would scurry along on the dining room floor, and I still remember one that was at least three inches long and an inch and a half wide. Everyone in the dining room got up and walked along following it. One man said, "Just a minute. Hold him here and I'll go get my saddle and I'll ride him."

The streets of Washington were filled with waves of groups of uniformed people, all handsome, beautiful in their classy-looking uniforms, and young, at the high pont of their calendar lives. They usually moved in groups which billowed here and there.

Everywhere in Washington, Bing Crosby was singing "White Christmas." You could have a beer in one place, move to another for a sandwich, and to yet another for dessert and never miss a syllable.

Our camaraderie was, naturally, phenomenal. Many endearing friendships flowered there, but always with the threat of impermanence and the unknown.

III
Assigned to the Land Down Under

Almost as a shock, almost unbelievably, came word one day that transportation had been found and that I was to leave in one half hour for Australia. The tension and suspense of living five months on a one-half-hour alert suddenly showed what such stress can do to a person, and the shock of this news was almost too great to bear. Still, I packed and was ready with one-half of a minute to spare, and boarded a troop train which was to carry us, thousands of us, with all window shades drawn, across the continent. Of course other troop trains were making the same journey, but from west to east instead.

My carry-on luggage was something for the comic strips, and what got checked through to the baggage department would have made my recruiting officer scream, "MOST, MOST HIGHLY IRREGULAR!" and then fall into a faint. I had decided I had to go my own way in regard to luggage. The Red Cross people had said over and over that they could give us no clues, no materials whatsoever, in planning recreation activities for combat troops in their camps. The situations and conditions were absolutely unpredictable, and we would have to wing it. I could not envision myself setting up any recreation program with nothing to work with. My presence with the men would have virtually been the same as not being there at all. With that in mind, I spent all my meager salary buying a second footlocker and stocking it with recreation supplies, and I pushed the luggage through every baggage handling station en route using every ounce of persuasion I could muster. What most people do not know is that this pliant, docile, agreeable little doll has a whim of iron which she uses reluctantly, and only in the most dire circumstances. I felt that this situation warranted whatever action I would have to take.

What does one stock in such a footlocker? I bought two dozen packs of playing cards, a half-dozen sets of pinochle cards, two card game instruction books, three books of instructions for other games, six checkerboards with checkers, equipment for several other table board games, six boxes of dominoes, twelve songbooks, three hymnals, a Bible, a dozen Victrola records, and a mouth organ. I also tucked in six yards of red plaid gingham and another two yards of a brilliant orange, yellow and green striped seating canvas. Then, too I added a guitar, which, of course, I would have to carry personally.

At every baggage depot, I explained to the military man in charge the reason for the extra footlocker. I received remarkably kind cooperation, but I did have to put up a polite fight at one station. The baggage master said, "You have your nerve! General MacArthur himself doesn't have clearance for two footlockers!"

Keeping my cool, I answered, "General MacArthur doesn't have to furnish recreation for troops stranded interminably in the boondocks! The military has requested the Red Cross to station recreation workers in these camps because, living in those almost totally deprived conditions, troops were becoming so depressed that many had to be evacuated to the United States for long-term psychiatric hospital care."

The baggage master thanked me and said, "I know what you mean."

I answered, "How would you like to be stationed in the camp where this request to the Red Cross was first made—in the Aleutian Islands?"

He answered, "I can hardly bear to think of it. God bless you, Miss Jones."

As I mentioned, this supply took all my salary. Never let it be said that Red Cross squanders even one penny of its donated money. We were reimbursed for expenditures for absolute necessities so long as they remained within Red Cross guidelines, and the guidelines were very skimpy, down to the last postage stamp. I had one-fifth of my salary sent automatically to a money manager in Milwaukee who was to pay any of my bills which could not be taken care of in advance, such as insurance, etc., but she managed to embezzle all I was so carefully laying aside. When I returned home years later, I discovered that she had been placed in a mental institution and there was no way of recouping my losses. Through all of those five years, I spent all the rest of my salary providing needed recreational-type items for servicemen. How could I not? Remember, MEET THE NEED!

Needless to say, I was the last of our Red Cross contingent to board the troop train. I should have been photographed, coat over my shoulder, handbag and overnight case in one hand, steel helmet and mess kit in the other, and on my back the guitar.

Our Red Cross staging station was San Francisco, and a group of four of us shared a hotel room there for two weeks, building four wonderful friendships: Betty Thompson, Laura (Tibby) Thibideau, Priscilla Naecker, and I. Of course we were scattered to assignments, far, far away from each other, but—*c'est le guerre.*

IV
Crossing the Pacific Pacific

I was sent to Balboa, the port of San Diego, and climbed onto a Swedish merchant vessel which carried twenty-four Red Cross workers, including the head of the American Red Cross in Australia, Charles Gamble, his wife, Vida, twenty Soviet citizens, several Australian and American businessmen, and 300 Dodge trucks.

The Pacific was mercifully pacific; an unexpected bonus. I had suffered all my life from motion sickness and fully expected to feed the fishes during the entire voyage. I did become so violently seasick while crossing the Tasman Sea as we neared the Australian coast that I had to be anesthetized, and awakened only as we approached Sidney lying prostrate and clad in Mrs. Gamble's silk nightgown. I thanked her profusely and told her I would wash it and return it to her, but she apparently thought the nightgown had had it by then and she graciously refused. I still have it among my souvenirs.

The voyage lasted four long weeks. Our Red Cross group, of course, developed a strong bond of friendship although we knew that, as usual, we would be scattered far and wide once we received our assignments.

The Soviet contingent was very interesting, made up of well-educated, promising, capable young people in their twenties. They were sent to enlarge the staff of the Soviet Consulate in Australia. We engaged them in conversation constantly, comparing notes on two subjects: world history and conditions among populations throughout the world. We discovered that world events, the way we had been taught, happened in far different ways when written by Soviet "historians." We were astounded to discover that even the simplest issues and happenings of history had been turned into the most amazing and alarming propaganda. Their consulate staff was being expanded to make up a staff larger than the staffs of the largest ambassadorships in the world. People who had had little or no experience with Soviet propaganda were amazed and could not bring themselves to believe what was really happening, but I had been the target of so many attempts to recruit me into Communism that I recognized the effort to woo me for what it was. Years later, in speaking of this to the man who had become my husband, a Finance Officer who had also been a Colonel in the secret Army Intelligence Corps, I was told that at the end of the war the Communists were making a strong attempt to take over the entire United States military with their "bore from within" tactics, and I saw many examples of this effort back in the States as the war wound down.

The American and Australian businessmen aboard ship were affable and pleasant traveling companions. One Australian in particular, Mr. Whitten, was returning from a mission of arranging war contracts with American manufacturers. He was a gentle, modest man, and he made the mistake of telling us a story one night. We young women were so enchanted with his manner and with his Australian cockney accent, which was totally new to us, that we were consumed with laughter. Thereafter, every night we would ask him to repeat the story. Laughter followed no matter how many times he told it. He was a dear and he knew that we all appreciated him.

This is his story: "When Oi waws about to leave Amerrica, one of the manufacturrrorrs gyve me ahs a fahwell gift a bottle of elegant brahndy. Oi felt thaht Oi'd bet-ta 'ave it ahnaloized befoh givin' it precious cahgo spice. The report read:'Your 'oss [horse] has diabetes.'"

How does one while away the hours of a four-week voyage across the Pacific? I couldn't just sit there and do nothing, so I asked the captain to let me help in any way whatever. I was amazed at what helpful activity he thought of: Would I like to be a helmsman for a four-hour shift each day? Well, yes. Of course! Before I knew it, I was standing at the helm, steering that ship four hours a day across the Pacific Ocean. Who, even in her wildest dreams, would ever have believed it? The steering wheel lay horizontally on a pedestal just at chest height. Just beneath the wheel was a wide circle divided into a multitude of minute divisions carefully numbered around the outer perimeter. A long needle was attached to the wheel, and that needle had to be kept exactly on one of those tiny marks on the dial, as determined each morning by the captain. I thought that I was doing a pretty fair job of it, but he told me at the end of the voyage that on my watch the wake of the ship consisted of a nervously wavering line. Oh well, he didn't take me off the job, did he? However, mine was a very useful effort, for it freed a crewman for a four-hour stint scanning the horizon with binoculars to spot, perish the thought, the periscope of any possible enemy submarine. We were not following a standard shipping lane because of submarine danger, and I wonder now how we all could have walked, without hesitation, right into the possibility of confronting those very jaws of death. You just do it, that's all. The captain and a crewman plotted the exact location of the ship every sunrise and sunset by a process of triangulation which only a mathematician can understand.

Another service which I graciously performed was darning a pillowcaseful of socks for the first mate.

The ship's officers were charming and gracious Swedes. They taught us three Swedish toasts as we lifted a glass of wine at dinner every night. "Skol!" was the first and simplest, and the meaning of this, as everyone knows, is: "Cheers," or, "Here's to you!" Another, and most delightful one, "Dien skol, mien skol, ala vacka flika skol," which means, "Here's to you, here's to me, here's to every pretty girl." The third one is a long, popular drinking song. With glass raised in hand, everyone sang, "Hel lon gore. Shung hope fa la ra, fal la ra lon lay." Now a big swallow. This continued, with song, then a big swallow, and then a rousing finale of the song, and then you drink it down. (I can't guarantee the spelling of these toasts, and not even the Swedish Consulate could help me.)

The first mate told this one: A circus came to a remote area of Sweden and an elephant got loose and strayed into the garden of a farmer and his wife. The woman, who had never seen an elephant, screamed to her husband, "Olaf, der iss a big annimule in de garrden puuulling up all de wegge-tables wit his tail!"

"What is he doing wit de wegge-tables?" said Olaf.

"If Iii tole you, you would neeever believe me!!"

All things come to an end, and so, too, did the voyage, without a hitch and, praise God, never a submarine sighted.

V
Getting Introduced to a Strange New Country

Entering Sydney's magnificent harbor is one of a lifetime's great experiences. Various fingers of land extend into the ocean, each providing natural docking. A wide bay in the center provides a spectacular panorama. A dramatic bridge spans the main harbor. Australians spoke often of "our 'arbor and our bridge" with great pride.

We passengers followed the usual wartime routine. Many friendships had developed. Strangely, they have a way of quickly becoming more intense than in relaxed peacetime conditions. We said goodbye and went our various ways. In wartime everything is temporary.

Four of us Red Cross women were brought to a hotel to await assignment in a week or possibly a fortnight. (See, I'm already becoming an Aussie. They say "fortnight" every chance they get.)

We arrived at our hotel at 3:30 P.M., just in time to be invited by the desk clerk to stop for a "spot o' tea" before going to our room. We were delighted for this opportunity to immediately take part in the great Australian ritual of afternoon tea.

We had hardly become seated around the tea table when we were approached by a handsome, pleasant Australian Army officer inquiring if he could join us. This was just one of our experiences with the outgoing friendliness of the Australian people. He told us he was in Sydney on Army business and was about to report back to his unit on location outside the country.

He asked if we would like him to fill us in with the basics of understanding Australia, which would help us to feel at home there in a very short time. We were delighted.

England originally used Australia as a penal colony, and nearly every Australian is descended from convicts. On completion of their sentences, the convicts were released to fend for themselves in this strange new land. Exploration was slow, always on foot and fraught with hardship.

Australia is roughly the same size and shape of the continental United States. The cities of Australia are located on the coastal perimeter, where climatic conditions are most suitable for living. A few miles inland from the east coast rises a range of mountains, spectacular to the Australians, but quite low to us Americans, called the Great Dividing Range. They extend the length of the east coast of the continent. A river about one-fourth as long as, and with probably one-tenth of the water of the Mississippi ambles through these mountains in a generally southwesterly direction and empties into the Pacific Ocean at Adelaide. This is the only real river of any size in the entire continent. It is called the Murray River, and it is joined by a lesser branch, the Darling, which flows into it from the northeast. Thus, it is understandable that when people talk with you, one of the first things they say is, "We need water." There was one "scheme" (hydroelectric power plant) in the Great Snowies, but that was all. It was understandably difficult for new settlers to cross the mountainous area, low as the mountains were, into the interior, and the released convicts suffered many hardships.

Inland from the eastern coastal cities and the Great Dividing Range, there is a wide strip of poorly watered bushy growth and woodland called the Bush. Inland from this is an area called the Outback, with even less rainfall, and then the Far Outback, with still less. Next comes the central part of the continent, the Great Australian Desert, similar in size and shape to the Sahara.

The climates of this continent range from Mediterranean to deep tropical. Melbourne, the largest city on the southeast coast, enjoys a climate similar to that of Los Angeles. The climate becomes warmer as one goes northward through Sydney and north to Brisbane nearing the Tropic of Capricorn, which marks the beginning of the tropics. People call this a subtropical climate, and as one travels farther northward, he gradually enters the deep tropics. The extreme northeast corner of the continent has a rainy deep tropical climate, the only part of Australia that has it. Darwin, at that time the only city on the northwest coast, is only eleven degrees (990 miles) from the Equator and has a dramatically intense monsoon climate, with six months of "the wet" and six months of "the dry." This climate extends down through most of the Northern Territory.

It is strange to realize that a continent of this large size contains only five states: Victoria, New South Wales, Western Australia, South Australia, and Queensland, and one large Northern Territory governed by Australia's national government.

Our newfound friend, in telling us these things, said that if we knew these few facts we could get along anywhere in the country, and he proved to be right. He also said that Australian speech is a result of the fact that except for a few doctors, businessmen, and highly trained specialists who came from England in fairly recent times, every Australian is a descendant of convicts, and that a large portion of them were scraped up from the streets of London within the sound of the bells of Bow Cathedral and spoke a heavy cockney dialect. This dialect has become the standard language of Australia, watered down into a mercifully understandable jargon. The deep, pure cockney of England is so guttural and garbled that one has to take college courses in cockney to understand it.

Our friend told us that his parents came from England to set up an export-import business. They sent him back to English boarding schools, and that was why he spoke without the cockney accent. Australians without the accent have had somewhat similar backgrounds.

To understand what Australians are saying, we need to realize that they pronounce vowels and diphthongs differently from the way we do. Long *a*, as in *day*, is pronounced as long *i*, so *day* to us is *die* to them. Our long *i* becomes *oi* to them. They tell us that they soften our short *a*, and they tell us that they are softening some of our other pronunciations. They drop the *h* from the beginning of words and roll their *r*'s. None of this means anything to us without practice. This is why our friend gave us three memorable examples of Australian pronunciation. (He unwittingly, also, tipped us off that much of the Australian humor is just a bit raunchy compared to what is considered polite and acceptable in America.)

He started us out gently with a riddle: "Waut's the difference between a buffalo and a bison?" Of course one does not know, so he replied, "A bafhalo is the animal on the Amerrrican foive-cent piece, but a bison is wa Oi wash me fice in."

Next, he told us the story of the wonderful Australian speller who entered an international spelling contest held in the United States. All his Australian friends were sure he would come home with the gold medal, but he flunked out early in the contest. Asked whatever happened, he replied, "Wen Oi firrst goht theah, Oi waws astawnded at 'ow dirrty thaose jolly Amerikans tawked. Thy kept sying, 'Under wot ossipisses arr yew 'erre?' Then cayme the cawntest, and 'ow waws Oi t'knaoow the jolly Amerricans spell 'oss piss: *eye-yew-s-p-oi-c-e?*"

Our friend's third illustration of cockney was even more illuminating. A new Army inductee from the Outback was being given a cursory physical examination. The doctor asked, "Werre yew cawnsti-pie-ted?"

"Aw, Gorr, no! Oi inlisted!" replied the soldier.

"Aw deah, we'll troy it anothah wye: 'Aw arr yourr bawels?'"

"Oi wawsn't issued any."

"No, man, 'ow are your bawels?"

"Oh! Me bawels: *eye, e, oi, oh,* and *yew.*"

"Oh, merrcy! This is terrrrible! 'E'll neverr do forr the Arrmy. 'E'll not be eyeble to read instructions. We'll 'ave to put 'im in a worrk de tye'l. 'E doesn't even know tha King's English. Tike 'im awye."

"Oi dew tew knows e's English! 'E is, 'e is, 'e is English."

"Oi dew feel just tha least bit guilty. Bring 'im back, we'll troy 'im once more, one lahst toyme. Dew yew 'ave sugar in your urine?"

"Dew Oi 'ave sugar in me urine? Aw Gorr no! Oi'm nawt such a bloody bloke! Oi awnly 'ave sugar in me tea."

I discovered afterward that if you could master these three stories, you could pretty well handle the Australian cockney speech, so he did us a favor in telling them to us.

A few minutes later our friend's driver arrived to take him to his duty location. A very sudden friendship had come to a quick, sudden wartime end. He said as he left, "I'll probably not be talking with ladies for some time," which I realized much later must have meant that he was going to the China-Burma-India theater.

We settled in for our fortnight's stay in Sydney. We decided to sample all the Australian customs we could, and one of the most delightful was early-morning tea. We were asked as we prepared to go to our room if we would like early-morning tea, and not wanting to miss a thing, we quickly said yes, and then had the presence of mind to ask what to expect. What we expected, and got, was a knock on the door at wake-up time and, with no further warning, the entrance of a maid carrying a tray of lovely hot tea and bread-and-butter sandwiches. This certainly wipes out the sleepy time cobwebs from one's mind in the most delightful way. When I get rich I'm going to have just such a maid in my mansion. Well, we can dream, can't we? The bread-and-butter sandwiches were so thin that I asked how a person could ever duplicate them. She told us that you start with a loaf of firm white bread, cut off the end crust, and with some soft butter spread the cut end of the loaf. Then you cut, with the sharpest knife to be found, the thinnest slice possible to mankind. You place the buttered side on another paper-thin slice from the loaf, do the appropriate trimming, and you have bread-and-butter sandwiches for early-morning tea.

We enjoyed all the other tea times of Australia. There is breakfast with tea. There is also morning tea, which is served at 10:30 to 11:00 A.M. There are even teaspoons which are slightly smaller than standard teaspoons called "elevenses." Morning tea usually consisted of a cup of tea and a biscuit, a biscuit being something between a cracker and a cookie, or possibly a scone, which as we all know is a glorified baking powder biscuit. A popular Australian term for pregnancy is "a scone in the oven." The beverage at lunchtime was tea, of course. Afternoon tea followed at 4:00 P.M. Like morning tea, it consisted of a cup or two of tea and a biscuit or scone. Every time I walked into a business establishment at ten-thirty or four during my whole stay in Australia, I was invited to a mug of tea and a biscuit taken from a nice tin biscuit box. Women in one-girl offices had their own equipment for boiling the water right in the mug—a hand-held electric heating element. Then there was "tea," and that meant the evening meal, or dinner, at about six-thirty or seven. As though that were not enough, when one was entertaining evening guests a pot of tea was beautifully presented, accompanied by some delightful dessert, usually a sponge cake. I think my dear Australians, nationwide, kept themselves on a constant tea jag.

We Red Cross women waiting for assignment decided to learn all we could about Sydney, and we explored the city on long walks. We went to the cinema—not the movies (you're in Australia now)—and we attended church. It seems strange at first to realize that there were, in general, only two churches one could attend. Often a colonial country is more English than the motherland; the only church one could attend was the Episcopalian, the Church of England. Well, not quite the only, for there were a few Roman Catholic churches. Catholics were so few and far between that someone might whisper, " 'E's an Rrr C. [Roman Catholic]."

One morning after I had commented that I felt that I was by then a dinky di native of Sydney, and just after the exquisite early-morning tea there came my orders to pack my bag and be ready to be picked up by 10:00 A.M. The familiar scenario of new friendships terminated by the impermanence of war was being reenacted once again.

VI

A Love Affair with Thousands

At long last, after half a year of waiting and filling in time, I had my assignment. I was to be a recreation worker with the Fifth and Seventh Regiments of the First Marine Division at Camp Balcombe and Mount Martha, near Melbourne, in the state of Victoria. My title was Able Bodied Recreation Worker, abbreviated in Red Cross parlance to Able Bodied Rec. So there I was on the train from Sydney in the state of New South Wales, which is a third of the way up the east coast, now bound for Melbourne in the southeast corner of the continent, complete with all my paraphernalia, including coat over my shoulder, handbag and overnight case in one hand, steel helmet and mess kit in the other, and on my back the good old guitar. Australian passenger cars were made up of small compartments opening to the outside, with few amenities. In some cases of urgency, it was necessary to use the steel helmet to relieve oneself. On other assignments, the helmet sometimes saved the day by becoming a washbasin, thoroughly scrubbed, of course, considering its possible previous use. I felt sorry

Lillian "Tillie" Jones with Marines from the Fifth and Seventh Regiments, Camp Balcombe, Australia—1942.

for civilian passengers on the train who did not have one. The train did stop at different stations en route, which were few and far between in this huge country. To top it off, on entering a new state everyone had to vacate the train and board a new train in the new state, baggage and all, because the distance between the rails, known as the gauge, was different in each state. We courageously made the shift as we entered the state of Victoria.

Camp Balcombe was a well-established Australian Army camp which they graciously vacated and turned over to the United States Marines. It was located forty miles south of Melbourne on one of several fingerlike peninsulas jutting southward into the ocean. It offered all the desired opportunities for Marine Corps amphibious and on-land training. The Fifth Regiment occupied Camp Balcombe, with its buildings of minimal structure, as befits an Army installation. The Seventh Regiment, however, was stationed at Mount Martha adjacent to it, but with all facilities housed in the ubiquitous pyramidal tents. A pyramidal tent is square with a canvas outer wall a little higher than a tall man's head. The roof section ascends from each canvas side wall to an upper point like a pyramid, thus the name pyramidal. Anywhere and everywhere in the military, the pyramidal tent housed the troops and business offices.

Officer Country at Camp Balcombe was made up of streets lined with corrugated galvanized iron huts which were used as offices of the regiment and sleeping accommodations for officers. There was also a large Officers' Mess Hall, a wooden structure used as dance hall and recreation room for the entire camp, and a surprisingly large wooden structure which was the camp hospital.

I was to work under the direction of Neil Bennett, a capable, imaginative, and cooperative man with the title of American Red Cross Assistant Field Director. Our office, of course, was in one of those small metal huts along the main street. There was also a hut for each of the chaplains; one was for the Protestant chaplain, named Ansgar Sovik, a genuine Scandinavian from Minneapolis. How could it be otherwise with a wonderful Scandinavian name like Ansgar Sovik? There was another hut for a quiet, effective Roman Catholic priest. Administrative offices completed Officers Row, followed by barracks/huts for officer housing.

My boss, Neil Bennett, introduced me immediately to the Marine Corps commander of the regiment, Col. Michael (Red Mike) Edson, a medium-statured, wiry, high-key, friendly, and extremely competent commanding officer. Neil asked his permission for me to serve as his assistant on the base, and Red Mike replied, "The Marines have never turned down a lady yet."

I was to eat most meals at the Fifth Regiment's Officers' Mess, and my toilet room, immediately shown to me, was to be the ladies' room in the basement of the dance hall. But where was I to sleep? There being no sleeping accommodations for ladies on the camp, a room was rented for me at a scaled-down version of a motel near the entrance to the camp. I was immediately issued a jeep for my own use and was duly installed there. I was in a little sleeping hut under a tree on the grounds, and what none of us knew but soon found out was that sleep was made nearly impossible by an occasional possum loosening her tail from its wraparound grip on a branch of the tree and thumping down on the cabin roof above me and by the incessant crawling and biting of bedbugs. This made it necessary to look farther afield for sleeping accommodations, and I rented half of a small double house in Mornington, a village four miles away, toward Melbourne. That jeep certainly turned out to be handy. It became a part of me. Although I left the house early every morning and returned at ten or later at night, including Saturdays, Sundays, and holidays, this quiet, comfortable sleeping space was an enormous comfort.

Lillian "Tillie" Jones with Chaplain Ansgar Sovik and some Fifth and Seventh Regiment Marines, Camp Balcombe.

There's a saying that you can go around the world to meet the guy next door. How true it is. The first person I met as I stepped foot on the soil of Camp Balcombe was, as I have mentioned, my Assistant Field Director, Neil Bennett, who introduced me to the camp commandant, "Red Mike," and he was immediately followed by an affable officer who told me his name and instantly announced, "You know, All Rightie died. Ruptured appendix." Although I did not know him, he knew me, his home being only two blocks from my apartment in Milwaukee, and All Rightie, to whom he was referring, was the salesperson in a high-quality bakery outlet located in the subbasement of my apartment building. Whenever any of her customers gave her an order, she'd answer, "All Rightie," as she turned to package it up. She was known throughout the community as All Rightie. No one even knew the real name of the bakery; we all just said we were going to buy something at All Rightie's. Poor, dear All Rightie, the neighborhood icon, dead and gone. God rest her soul. You can go around the world to meet the person next door!

Neil's and my first task was an assessment of the recreation needs of the two camps and a decision as to how best we could meet those needs. Bearing in mind the reason for the Marines' being in Camp Balcombe and Mount Martha, that of preparing for the liberation of some Japanese-held island farther north, Neil and I realized that there was no point in providing daytime weekday recreation. These servicemen were spending every weekday in

Lillian "Tillie" Jones in her jeep, Camp Balcombe, Mornington Peninsula, Victoria, New South Wales, Australia on Marine Corps camp—1942.

military drills and ever longer and more arduous training marches. We decided to look for other means of meeting their needs. One need was for me to visit the Marines who were in the hospital, nearly all of them suffering from malaria, a scourge of their previous action on Guadalcanal, but amenable to treatment in time to ready them for further action.

Another need was to provide weekend recreation. We decided that the best way to do this, given existing facilities and civilian community aid, was to run weekly dances for all the enlisted men in both regiments and to provide weekend overnight visits with Australian families on the peninsula.

Another need in these two large regiments was for some kind of a weekly newspaper. If I took on that task, I could, without its being obvious, become a big sister, confidante, and touch of home for these men, which turned out to be perhaps the best thing I did for them in such a stressful time.

These Marines had just returned, those of them still alive and able-bodied, from their colossal task of liberating the island of Guadalcanal from the Japanese, establishing it as a safe American-held island. I learned much later that its strategic location just off the eastern tip of New Guinea gave it, in American hands, the role of protecting American troops and supply ships nearing their landings in Australia. The liberation of Guadalcanal was the beginning of the rollback of Japan's aggressive territorial expansion aimed at creating a gigantic Japanese empire.

The Japanese, ruled by the military, with the Army in absolute control and the emperor only a figurehead, had set Japan on a course of aggressive territorial expansion southward. By 1930, they had wrested Manchuria, Korea, and Formosa from China and had been constantly encroaching on China's mainland, and now, beginning with the surprise attack on Pearl Harbor, they had taken our islands of Wake, Guam, and the Philippines. They had also taken about a third of China, and French Indochina, Hong Kong, Burma, the Malay Peninsula, Singapore, the Netherlands Indies, including Borneo, and northern New Guinea, had invaded eastern India, and had bombed Darwin in Australia. All this in five months' time! There was great apprehension lest they invade our United States mainland.

The Marines had been stationed temporarily, before landing at Guadalcanal, at a place called Pie-cock-a-reeky (don't ask me how to spell it), a muddy hole in New Zealand. A Marine had written a poem about it which ended: "Given a choice between there and hell, I'll take hell, and leave to you the mud at Pie-cock-a-reeky."

The task of the Marines on our two camps was to bring the regiments up to standard strength with new recruits and to train for a liberating assault on some other Japanese-held island farther north.

Although Neil Bennett took care of the Red Cross social work side of our services and handled Red Cross business matters, he was also an excellent right hand for me in recreation activities.

Our weekend dances proved to be very popular. The hall was filled at every dance. Young ladies came in many large groups to volunteer as dancing partners, and the "joint was jumping" all evening. At each of those evenings I danced for three hours without stopping, managing to dance with fifty or more enlisted men, and I never got tired. The jitterbug was the popular new craze, and one night an enthusiastic Marine threw my shoulder out of joint tossing me over his head to catch me coming down on his other side. It was only a temporary inconvenience, however, and I kept right on whooping it up with the rest of them. Those nights were great fun for everybody.

Overnight weekend visits to homes on the peninsula were very popular. We kept two long lists, one of servicemen wishing for an invitation, the other of Australian families offering to be hosts. This latter list was constantly replenished by these grateful Australians wishing to show their gratitude to their American saviors. Over and over they told us that were it not for the American presence, their country would surely have been invaded, for most Australian servicemen were fighting abroad in Europe, the China-Burma-India theater, New Guinea, and Borneo.

I responded to one such invitation and became the overnight guest of a family who happened to run a sheep station. What a bummer! It might have been, and probably was, a bummer, too, for my hosts.

I was housed in a tiny one-man bunk house on the outer edge of their crude courtyard, but I spent the better part of two days with the family in their barracks-type house. The house was a make-do barnlike means of camping in, with rough exposed beams, unfinished wooden walls, and wide plank floors. The crude furniture was completely in keeping with the harsh aspects of the interior. The food, too, matched this ambiance, and as for the family, they topped off the whole scene in perfect unison with the total environment. We sat for hours saying virtually nothing, with me making one unsuccessful sally after another into conversation that died in its tracks. These people were not surly, however, and did not appear to resent my presence even as a mere woman, and I wondered if their struggles to make a go of it in an often hostile land had perhaps made a costly imprint on their personalities. After all, they were showing a welcome to, and gratitude for, the American presence in their country in those times of mortal national danger. In their way, I am sure they were doing their best. It was a valuable visit for me because it showed me the vicissitudes and the harshness of life for many people in that huge country, a country of a very limited natural resources.

Another popular source of entertainment was Tokyo Rose's radio broadcasts. It was the best radio program around, and servicemen throughout the entire Pacific, particularly Marines and Navy men, wherever radio transmission was available, listened to it regularly. In this case the "commercials" were short conversational bits of Japanese propaganda, kept mild in order not to infuriate, and thus alienate, her listeners, but relying on constant propagandizing to accomplish their ends. She was charming, softly witty, sometimes joking, sometimes gently chiding, and always American in cultural background. She was almost a voice from home. Her program was the place where one could always hear the popular American music of the day: the big bands, popular choral groups and solists, singable and danceable, pleasant music. However, for all her popularity, I never heard a single person who believed a word she said. Everyone knew that for all its subtlety, it was out-and-out propaganda, and I never met a single servicemen whose morale or patriotic loyalty was diminished by Tokyo Rose.

There is an interesting twist to the story of Tokyo Rose. We all often wondered who she was and how she could be so Japanese but could seem almost to have been born an American, speaking perfect English with no accent whatever and using American figures of speech and current slang. No one but an American-born young woman could playfully tease and twit our troops with such skill—she must have been one of us. As a matter of fact, she was. I found out, after all these years, that she was Iva Ikuko Toguri, a Nisei, that is, daughter of Japanese parents who had emigrated from Japan to America. They lived in California, and she was a graduate of the University of California at Los Angeles with a major in zoology. She went to Japan to visit a sick aunt, arriving just before the beginning of the war, and on Pearl Harbor Day she became an enemy alien. She would have been sent to an internment camp to wait out the three and a half years of conflict but avoided this by volunteering to do English-language broadcasting for the Japanese. She broadcast every night, in her velvety bedroomlike voice, for a salary of six dollars and fifty cents a month until the end of the war. Her delightful musical recordings were probably discs obtained from neutral embassies in Tokyo. She was constantly telling our troops that the United States was losing the war, but her entire audience knew better. I wonder what her life was like after the war, don't you?

My partner, Neil Bennett, had asked me to publish a camp newspaper, which I willingly agreed to do. Much later, a Marine officer thanked me, saying it spared them the task and if I had not agreed to do it, they would have had to publish one themselves.

In my jeep I circulated through both Camp Balcombe and Mount Martha gathering news. It had to be done in the daytime, but this aspect was workable because there were always some Marines around who were not on a training maneuver.

Our first task was to run a contest to settle on a name, and we decided to call the paper the *Scuttlebutt Gazette. Scuttlebutt* was the perfect word, for it means gossip, "the word" that is passed around from one to another, be it a joke, a comment, a piece of almost secret news, a friendly caution, or just plain gossip. Orders and instructions, too, were passed around orally as an adjunct to written orders delivered to the men by their sergeants. There was a saying in camp that "there is always someone who doesn't get the word." Therefore, our *Scuttlebutt Gazette* also served as a means of passing "the word."

I found a cartoonist to prepare a masthead for each issue, and his sketches and the jokes or comments connected with them were wonderful attention getters.

I gathered the news, I wrote it, I typed it, I cut the mimeograph stencils, I ran them off on the mimeograph, I collated them, I stapled them, and while delivering them throughout both camps in my jeep I gathered news for the next week's issue.

While I was collecting my news stories, I was also learning about Marines and their life.

The Sergeants were something to behold. I watched them conducting military drill, and, wow, did I learn about command presence! In later years while back teaching at Milwaukee's South Division High School, I could call to order without a microphone four hundred raucous students and keep them quietly studying at their desks in study hall with the consummate skill of those sergeants, and they even liked it. How do you call a motley group to order? You march into the room in stiff military manner with the message "I am the boss" exuding from every pore, you rap on the desk or table with your gavel, and you say, "Atten-TION," or words to that effect. Looking them straight in the eye, you fix them with a glassy, cold stare, with ice water dripping every inch of the way. They'll calm down. You bet your boots they will! I have seen so many people in positions of leadership unable to accomplish this feat that I have often wished they could take a few days off to observe a Marine drill sergeant.

These sergeants were masters at leading the men in their precision marching. They had other duties as well because each one was in charge of his squad, made up of men in all phases of Marine Corps life. Of course the trick is to be able to relax and show friendly concern and moral support for each of them, which some sergeants, stepped in their leadership role, found hard, even impossible to do.

Another aspect of the Sergeant's value to his men was that of building individual initiative and mutual emotional support, thus achieving a cohesive and very effective military force. This expressed itself sometimes, however, as necessary "tough love." The men themselves were wonderfully supportive of each other. They helped one another, encouraged each other, and their devotion to one another was beautiful to behold. They would gladly give their lives for their comrades if necessary. This, of course, is the secret of morale. A demonstration of this tough love was shown to me several times, and I have never ceased to marvel at it. When some poor soul of an enlisted man would be weak enough to speak piteously of some hardship he had endured, he was sure to get the treatment. Let us say, for instance, that one of them might have said that on the last march his bedroll had become soaked when they forded the last creek and he hardly slept a wink all night trying to get comfortable on that cold, wet padding. This sad whimper would call out a group of his comrades who would stand in a row before him, legs spread, arms akimbo, and say loudly in unison and in mock pity, "Well, hain't that jist a goddamn shame!" You can bet that poor fellow would walk through burning coals before he would ever complain again.

People sometimes ask me what was the hardest thing I had to cope with in all my wartime experience. Believe it or not, it was nothing in the concrete world, but in the abstract. It was a word; one word, only one word, and that word was *fuck*. I could take all the rest of it: the occasional K rations, the powdered eggs, the flies, the mosquitoes, the long hours and no days off, not even Sundays or holidays, the feeling of always being alone in a strange land. I could take it all, but fuck all but did me in. Fuck was everywhere. No one could say three words without it. Everything was fuck, fuck, fuck. Fuck the rain, fuck the heat, fuck the jeep, fuck the rifle, fuck the mud, fuck you, fuck him, fuck it, fuck them, fuck the corporal, fuck the sergeant, fuck the trees, fuck the grass, fuck the water, fuck everybody, fuck anything you can name. What the fuck, where the fuck, how the fuck, who the fuck, when the fuck, why the fuck, oh the fuck! My fuckin' tie, my fuckin' shoes, the fuckin' lunch, the fuckin' mess, the fuckin' corporal, the fuckin' sergeant, the fuckin' road, the fuckin' ocean, the fuckin' flowers, the fuckin' chair, the fuckin' anything and everything. They also had two favorite acronyms, each of which condensed a whole *fuck* sentence into one word: SNAFU, meaning "situation normal, all fucked up," and TARFU, to indicate "things are really fucked up." One veteran of Guadalcanal told about a jeep driver being told by a guard to "turn out the fuckin' lights." The driver's response was, "I can't turn out the fuckin' lights. I've got the fuckin' Colonel!" One night after mess while I was at work on the *Scuttlebutt Gazette* in our office, I heard a couple of enlisted men who were on a walking excursion in Officers' Country say, "Here's a fuckin' label, right at this fuckin' door. What kind of a fuckin' name is this: 'Ansgar Sovik, Chaplain.' You don't 'spose he's a fuckin' Jew, do you?"

I had a hard time figuring out how to handle this word. I finally decided that since I was on the camp to help these men and not to harp at them to clean out their mouths, I would have to pay no attention to it, pass it off, let it go in one ear and out the other unless it was applied to me directly, in which case I didn't know how I could ever handle it. Worst came to worst a couple of years later when I worked at an R & R Navy camp. Standing to greet a busload of incoming men, I was accosted by one who blurted out, "I knew I was goin' to meet a fuckin' dame, but I didn't know I was goin' to meet a fuckin' dame like you!" That did it for me! Perhaps it was because I had by then lived in so many stressful situations that my tolerance level was in delicate balance, but this I couldn't stand, and as I walked off in tears, I heard him say, "Oh, what the fuck. I can't do one fuckin' thing right. What fuckin' thing have I said now? I only said I knew I was goin' to meet a fuckin' dame, but I didn't know I was goin' to meet a fuckin' dame like you. What the fuck. I might as well get back on the fuckin' bus and go back to the fuckin' base." Perhaps, though, I should count my blessings. I never once heard the sh——word, and there was surprisingly little use of *hell* and *goddamn*. If we look hard enough, we can usually find something to be thankful for.

Echoes of Guadalcanal

Although Marine casualties on Guadalcanal were alarmingly heavy, quite a few of its liberation troops survived to fight again and be killed later, farther north. Various surviving Marines told me anecdotes of their presence there. It would have been wonderful to have been able to tape them.

The Japanese fought fiercely. They considered it an honor to die. The battle of Guadalcanal, the first island to be liberated, took six terrible months. We lost three thousand Marines, but the Japs, who fought savagely, mainly from jungle hideouts and caves, were almost all killed, some killing themselves rather than being taken prisoner. Intense heat, tangled jungle growth, mosquitoes, malaria, dysentery, jungle rot, and rats all combined to make conditions virtually unbearable. The food was horrible, the Marines lived on condemned rations still being used as an economy measure. Lacking shipments of supplies, the Japanese lived on roots, bugs, and worms. The average Marine lost eighteen pounds; the average Japanese, forty.

I was fortunate to be able to interview for the *Gazette* M. Sgt. Lew Diamond, just days before he was to leave for the States, his many years of service in the Marines completed. Lew was a legendary figure of Guadalcanal, a Gunnery Sergeant admired by everyone. I asked him to tell me the story of his work at "The Slot," which his fellow Marines had talked about with great admiration.

The Slot was a narrow strait between the north and south islands of the Solomons group, of which Guadalcanal was one. The Japanese were building an airfield on Guadalcanal, the reason for choosing that island to liberate. The Slot led directly to the airfield and proved a perfect guide for a target. The Japanese flew over the Slot and up over the island to drop their bombs. However, the Slot served a double purpose. It provided a means of making each plane a perfect target because each one came in directly over the Slot, and Lew positioned his gun at just the right angle to shoot them down. The location of his gun was so perfectly camouflaged that the Japanese were never able to find it and put it out of commission. Lew became a legend with the Marines and it was a great honor for me to meet and talk with him. The airfield was named Henderson Field in honor of a dead war hero.

There are many strange quirks of war, and the following account describes one of the strangest quirks of all. A Marine, in chatting with me, told me the story of how the Guadalcanal airfield was taken and held by the Americans just before the Marines were to make their amphibious landing on the island. The airfield was on the opposite side of the island from Japanese encampments. The Japanese were so confident of their possession of the entire island, and the airfield in particular, that they did not bother to station guards there.

A U.S. Army company was dropped onto the airfield with orders to take the field and secure it from Japanese attack. The Lieutenant in charge was a "ninety-day wonder," having just finished the three-month, ninety-day officer training course, and had never been in battle. He turned to his Master Sergeant and said, "In God's name, what am I ever to do? How can I go about this?"

The Sergeant answered, "You know, of course, that I am a seasoned combat veteran of World War I, but what most people don't know is that ever since, I have studied military tactics as a hobby. Do you want me to do this job for you?"

"Oh, would you?" pleaded the Lieutenant.

"Are you willing to be just one of the men?" asked the Sergeant.

"Oh, yes, yes, anything!"

The Sergeant called the men together and told them they had only a few minutes to complete their plan and must expect a Japanese attack almost immediately. He told them to take places around the perimeter of the field and to be sure to hide themselves completely. They were to fire, one by one, in rotation, thus giving time after shooting to reload their rifles and/or be ready to do anything necessary to be ready to shoot again, and they were not to fire until a Japanese soldier stepped onto the airfield and paused to look around for someone to shoot. That would be the signal for the next man in rotation to fire.

The Japanese came almost immediately, as predicted, one after another stepping onto the field, looking around for someone to shoot, and being shot dead instead. They came and came, closely following each other, climbing over their dead to get onto the field. By the time their attack ended, their bodies lay in piles, one on top of another. And what of the American casualties? There were none. Not one!

Colonel Edson, "Red Mike," arrived shortly after, the Marines having made a successful amphibious landing. He put his arm around the Army Sergeant's shoulders and exclaimed, "You'd make a hell of a swell Marine. I'm going to recommend you for the Congressional Medal of Honor!" To tell a man he'd make a hell of a swell Marine was unbelievably extravagant praise, since about the most complimentary thing you could say to any Marine was that he was a good Marine.

A decade or so later when my husband, a retired Army Captain, and I were talking one evening, I asked him to tell me how he won the Distinguished Service Cross in World War I and again in World War II. The Distinguished Service Cross is only one step below the Congressional Medal of Honor. As the evening went on and he began to tell me how he won this decoration in World War II, he told me the same story. He himself had been that Army Master Sergeant who had directed the U.S. capture of the Guadalcanal airfield! My own husband! Did you ever hear of a stranger quirk of war?

My news gathering served another, most significant purpose. What I was doing in these conversations with the men was purposely never named or articulated, but as I have mentioned, through these talks I became their friend, their confidante, their big sister, a touch of home. In retrospect, I feel that my greatest contribution and most significant value to them was in helping them cope with their overriding, all-consuming apprehension: the likelihood of almost certain death and the need to gather the strength to face death fearlessly and unflinchingly. It seems to me now that all else I did all those seven months was only secondary.

Somewhere in all the conversations with these men, I emphasized that they could tell me anything, no matter what it was, without worrying about shocking me, nor about confidentiality. I would absolutely never, in God's world, repeat a confidence. They began coming to me just to talk, and talk they did. These survivors of Guadalcanal had been subjected to the untold stress of living as raw campers on a tropical jungle island for six months, in constant misery and expectancy of being killed. They had been subjected to unbelievable trauma, and talking about it could often relieve them from some of the stresses of their horrible memories. New recruits, too, had their stresses of coming to terms, as did the Guadalcanal survivors, with the possibility, indeed tremendous likelihood, of being killed in their next invasion action. Facing this terrifying prospect, they poured out their hearts to me. Each talk centered on three successive topics: how they felt about their lives so far; how they felt about Guadalcanal, those who had fought there; and how they could face their terrible future.

At the beginning of each of these visits I would tell them I was getting out my (imaginary) crying towel and, in pantomime, drape it across my shoulder, telling them it was embroidered with the words FOR CRYING. This started us off on an easygoing, somewhat happy note and, my word, what confidences I heard!

The enlisted men were young, some of them eighteen or nineteen years old, and many in their very early twenties. They told me stories of their hometowns, their families, their school days, and their girlfriends, and, some of them, of their marriages. I am, to this day, amazed at two regrets which absolutely all, every last one of them, confessed sadly. The first was, "I wish I had worked harder at being a better student." The other was, "I wish I had been a better son to my mother."

In talking about Guadalcanal, these men did not dwell on the hardships of life there, the tropical heat, the mosquitoes, the malaria, dysentery jungle rot, the terrible rations, sleeping on a bedroll, and all other creature discomforts. Never once did a single one say he was sorry he was risking his life, and I always thanked them in my heart for such self-sacrifice. They told me many accounts of incidents there. One thing, though, that many of them talked about was their struggle in summoning the courage to walk fearlessly into the very face of death. One of them put it very graphically when he said, "I couldn't bring myself to do it until I happened to see General Vandegrift, Commandant of the Marine Corps, walk right through enemy fire without batting an eye. I said to myself, *If he can do it, I can do it.*" Incidentally, I learned that one of the chief tasks of an officer is to walk fearlessly through enemy fire, thus setting an example for those who follow.

Some told me of messages they were sending home to loved ones in case it would be the last one they would ever send. What touching confidences!

Two Marines did, each, tell me a horror story which haunts me even now, after all these years. The first one, choking the words out, said that he had shot and killed his Sergeant, who was walking in front of him during action on Guadalcanal. "He was mean to us, terribly mean. We all hated him. But now I feel terrible about it. What on earth shall I do?"

I clasped him to me and he wept on my crying towel, sobbing out, "What can I do? What can I do?"

I asked him to give me a little time to think. Of course, one should turn in a murderer, but I was on the horns of a horrible dilemma. I had sworn absolute confidentiality. How could I break that promise? Should I tell him to turn himself in? Should I tell him to tell this to his chaplain? But I was, in effect, his chaplain that day. I finally figured out a workable suggestion. I told him, "We know this is a terrible burden of guilt for you to carry, but there is also a way that you can make it right. We know you are going into battle again, and you can save the lives of comrades in some terrible situation which no one else can bring himself to tackle."

He said, "Yes! You've given me an idea. Thank you; thank you!" He dried his tears and left visibly relieved.

The one other enlisted man who told me of such an incident repeated the same story virtually word for word, with his horrible guilt racking his very soul. I told him that same thing, and he expressed his gratitude at helping him to discover a solution to his horrible dilemma. I found out much later that both of these men had done exactly that. They had, with unbelievable self-sacrifice in their next battle action, saved the lives of fellow Marines, but were killed doing it. I have been carrying around this burden ever since. Should I have turned in both of the Marines who made this confession to me, or did I give them the right advice? What would you have done?

Sir Harold's Hospital

Traditionally, ministering to the sick is the first duty, perhaps the paramount duty, of the Red Cross. The hospital was the only facility at Camp Balcombe still run by Australians. The man in charge of the hospital was "Sirrrr Harrrrold Zshongoo Smith, Thrice Mayor of Melbourne!" (How does one spell Zshongoo?) This pompous piece of humanity could never forget, even in his sleep, the importance of his past and present exalted positions, and he was determined that no one else would forget it either. He strutted around the premises wearing a monocle and carrying a riding crop to let everybody know of his supreme eminence. His uniform included short khaki pants reaching to just above the knee, with wide, floppy legs which made everyone who wore them cooler but definitely less visually attractive. He had an assistant who was appropriately quiet, respectful, and subservient, dressed in the same garb. One day a goat which ambled at will through the camp approached this hapless aide from the rear, pushed its head between his legs, and gave him a ride on its shoulders. Thank heaven I happened to be some distance behind him and he never knew that I witnessed his inglorious debasement. I couldn't help wondering how it would have looked with Sirrr Harrold Zshongoo Smith, Thrice Mayor of Melbourne, on the goat's shoulders instead!

The hospital, of rough but adequate architecture, staffed entirely by Australians, was large and contained many wards, nearly all of them filled with bedridden Marines, most of them suffering from malaria, a hideous scourge they had brought with them from Guadalcanal. However, they could respond well to treatment and go back on duty.

Although I was assigned to the Officers' Mess for meals, weekday lunchtime created a problem because the officers were always away on training duties, so lunch was not served there. It was decided that I eat lunch alone at a table in the hospital kitchen. I was not completely alone, however, because the cook, an older Australian woman, was shuffling about on her kitchen duties. The food was unspeakable. Day after day I was served up a plate of some unpromising edibles, accompanied always by a large slab of boiled pumpkin, absolutely unaided by any taste enhancer. I worked valiantly on this unappetizing viand but at last had to consider giving it up entirely. One day, though, in an effort to continue my growing friendly rapport with this elderly lady, I asked her why she didn't retire and take up a pleasant rocking chair life, which I was sure she had by now earned many times over. She replied with a war story I shall never forget: "Me 'usband's dead from World War I injuries, and me foive sons are all somewhere in China or Burma or India or New Guinea or Borneo. Oi 'aven't 'eard a word from a one of them in over a year, and if Oi didn't 'ave me job, Oi would lose me moind." I stood up, put my arms around her, and she wiped her eyes with the corner of her apron. After that, boiled pumpkin tasted a little better and I ate it gallantly every day. Sometimes I even began to think it tasted a bit like something to eat.

The nurses in the hospital wore the nursing uniform of England: a gray cotton cambric shirtwaist dress and a white cloth headpiece which formed a band around the forehead and temples and flowed out to a short capelike flare in the back, just touching the shoulders in length. A large red fabric cross in the center of the headpiece identified them. The entire uniform was quite attractive.

The nurses did a marvelous job. They virtually ran the hospital. When you come right down to it, isn't it always the nurses who run the hospitals? They are the omnipresent, effective caregivers worldwide. One nurse, Sister Jackson, I shall always remember with love, admiration, and gratitude. She always went the extra mile in caring for those sick men on her wards, always kindly, always there with extra, thoughtful attentions. The men loved her. Besides being a medical caregiver and morale booster, she was easy to talk with. The Marines practiced her cockney dialect, and she applauded them for it. The rapport was beautiful to see. One afternoon Sister Jackson announced that she would not be there the next day because she was taking a one-day " 'olidye." In Australia, if a person had one day or one hundred days off duty it was called a holiday. The men told her they would miss her but wanted her to have a good time, and the holiday duly took place.

The next morning, poor Sister Jackson rushed into my office in tears. "Wot 'ave Oi said? Wot 'ave Oi said? Every toime Oi enter that ward the men scream with laughter, pound the pillows, and just about collapse."

I said, "Oh, Sister Jackson, they love you. You know that. There must have been some innocent remark that set them off. Tell me everything that happened."

She then explained: "The very firrst moment Oi entered the warrd this morrnin', thy called out in a chorrus, 'Aw waws yourr jawlly 'olidye, Sister Jackson?' Oi answered that it was teddible! Simply teddible! In tha firrst plyce, when Oi got to tha trrahnsporrt depot, therre waws no prroperr passengerr automobile and Oi 'ad to roide those forrty moiles into Melbourne in a lorrrry. The roide waws so rough Oi waws nerrly shyken aparrt. To mike matterrs wurrse, the lorrrry stopped at the trahnsporrt deppot a moile from Melbourne and Oi 'ad to walk tha rest of tha wye. Oi 'ad six imporrtant pieces of business to tyke carre of, including a doctorr's appointment, but couldn't get 'em done becaws eitherr the storres were out o' stock, orrr tha perrson tyking carre of wawt Oi needed 'ad gone into the serrvice. Tha only thing Oi did get accomplished waws tha doctorr's appointment. Couming 'ome waws the syme storry, tha moile wawk to the trrahnsporrt depot, and tha rough roide back in tha lorrry, AND OI'M FAIRR KNOCKED UP! Then one of those sick men sat roit up in bed, shook 'is fist, and shouted, 'OO'S THE BLOODY BLOKE? OI'LL SHOOT 'IM!' "

At this she cried even more, and as she wiped her tears I said, "Oh, darling Sister Jackson, the men love you and you know that, but you've just told them that as a result of back alley fornication you're pregnant!" The torrent of tears changed into tears of hysterical laughter, and we both went back to the ward, where I explained to the men that in Australia when you're knocked up, it simply means that you're totally exhausted. We all laughed even more and the world once again turned on its axis.

In their desire to do their part to help the Americans, the ladies of the Mornington Peninsula turned out in large numbers as Australian Red Cross to minister to the needs of these sick men. They were wonderful, and many of them became my very dear friends. They cosseted the men, pampering them to a point where some of them confided to me that if it were all the same with the Colonel, they would just as soon remain in the hospital. The ministrations of these wonderful women lightened my work immensely, for otherwise I would have had to spend a very large part of my time with the hospitalized Marines and, in so doing, neglect the able-bodied.

One day some remarkable news was imparted to us: Eleanor Roosevelt was going to spend a day visiting Camp Balcombe and Mount Martha! We had several days' notice, which gave us time to slick up our environs and ready ourselves to welcome her, and that's where I came in. The new colonel (we called him Colonel John) paid me a special visit to tell me that that Eleanor was to be first treated to a Marine-type landing in an amphibious tractor, inching through the water and then up onto terra firma, making her first step onto dry land. She was then to be granted her wish to talk personally with Captain McIlhenny, whose family owned New Iberia Island, off the coast of Louisiana, where they made Tabasco sauce. His relatives had particularly asked her to look him up. She was then to have lunch with the officers at their mess hall. At the end of the luncheon, would I please show her to the ladies' room? In preparation for this auspicious duty, I scrubbed that ladies' room day after day until I could scrub no more, and on the morning of the visit I brought down a water glass filled with some Australian wildflowers which doubled themselves in the mirror above the vanity shelf.

Inviting Eleanor Roosevelt to the Ladies' Room, Officers' Mess, Fifth Regiment, First Marine Division, Camp Balcombe, Mornington Peninsula, 4 miles from Melbourne, Victoria, New South Wales, autumn—1942.

The Melbourne newspapers showed great admiration for Eleanor as she visited the huge new hospital which the Melbourne people had turned over to the United States military. She had shaken hands and talked with each of the ninety sick American servicemen there the day before she visited us.

All went well with her visit to our camp, and I dutifully played my part by inviting her to the ladies' room. The photographer caught this solicitous conversation on film and several years later, back in San Francisco, I had Christmas cards made with this picture to send to relatives and friends but then was too busy to send them. Eleanor's descent into the haven of femininity and her return were so swift it should have been in the *Guinness Book of Records.* I am sure she never had a moment to view the pristine cleanliness and floral beauty of my lovely toilet room!

Following the luncheon, our First Lady paid a visit to the hospital. I escorted her there, where the whole event was officiously taken over by you know who: Sirr Harrold Zshongoo Smith, Thrice Mayor of Melbourne, complete with short, wide pants, monocle, and riding crop. The wonderful Australian volunteer Red Cross ladies stood thrilled, at rigid attention, all in a row. Unfortunately, no photographer came to preserve the great moment in pictures. This was an enormous disappointment to the ladies, and some years later when I was back at home and at work again in Milwaukee, Eleanor happened to visit our city. I was able to get her to send them a large portrait of herself on which she wrote: "With great appreciation to the volunteer ladies of the Australian Red Cross, Mornington Peninsula, Australia."

The day after Eleanor's visit to our camp, our dear Colonel John came to my office to thank me for my contribution, which he said was of strategic importance to the whole operation, and with a comical smile he asked, "Was everything all right below?"

The comradeship the Australian Red Cross ladies extended to me was a high point of my whole war experience. Various ones of them invited me to their homes and gave me the personal friendships so important in rounding out one's life. Thus, I did not have to just be with men, only men, all the time and all the time—a surprisingly lopsided life.

One interesting family lived a strangely divided existence, with the wife and children living comfortably and pleasantly in a lovely home in Mornington and the husband away most of the time operating a vast sheep station quite some distance away and giving himself a "holiday" at home from time to time. This lady showed me around her home, including a workroom on the first floor inhabited by a bedraggled woman bent over a washboard, her arms up to her elbows in the strong soapsuds of the washtub. My hostess introduced her as her washlady, explaining to me that she worked two eight-hour days a week for this lady and piled her occupation with other families four more days a week. Upon observing my astonishment at the lack of household machinery in this modern age, they explained that without adequate facilities for electric power, much work still had to be done by hand and that not every family found it feasible to install and operate a private coal or gasoline-driven home power plant, and even if they did, wartime shortages of fuel would make even this impossible. How would you like to be such a worker? If that isn't earning your living the hard way, nothing is.

One most memorable visit came when Bunny Watts invited me for an evening with her and her husband, who, incidentally, was a direct descendent of James Watts, the inventor of the steam engine. Bunny and her husband appeared to be very wealthy and they lived a decidedly English style of life in a lovely commodious but unpretentious home. As we sat enjoying highballs in their beautiful living room an hour before dinner, their nanny walked in with their young son of about two years of age for his one hour's daily visit with his parents. All the rest of the time he lived in a separate apartment with the nanny. This amazed me, it being my first introduction to English nanny-hood. Later, we exchanged descriptions of our days: Mr. Watts told us of his, I described my days at the camp, and Bunny told of her days as a wealthy, albeit modest and unassuming, matron. Bless them, these dear people never spoke of or flaunted their wealth, though to even the casual observer it was plainly evident. Her first morning duty consisted of going through the garden clipping spent blooms, picking flowers for vases, and replenishing the vases in the home. She spent many, many hours in wonderful unpaid volunteer services in the community. She was an excellent cook and had personally prepared our dinner, the entrée of which consisted of a delicious rabbit stew.

After dinner, Bunny proudly showed me a most remarkable piece of kitchen equipment. I can see it now—a fabulous Swedish-made cookstove. All cooking in Australia was done on cookstoves in the absence of hydroelectric and/or gas supplies countrywide. Her stove, of beautiful polished black cast iron, sported a remarkable collection of cooking areas, each marked off by the usual removable round lid. Each one remained at a steady temperature all day and night, and each one was of a different temperature from every other one. This made it possible to cook any food you wanted, at any temperature you wanted. It was fueled by a small stove shovelful of coke, amounting to about a one-pint quantity once a day. "What an engineering triumph!" I exclaimed in wonderment, and wished aloud that every Australian family could have one. Then I asked her how they got it and what it had cost. They had imported it directly from Sweden and it had cost them the equivalent of fifteen hundred dollars, which made it unaffordable to nearly everyone. When one factors in fifty years of inflation, one realizes that the cost was the equivalent of what, at that time, amounted to many thousands of dollars. I have often thought that it would have paid the Australian government to buy them wholesale in great quantities and sell them, even at a loss, to the populace, thus helping enormously to lessen the unbelievable erosion caused by uprooting trees and brush, using both branches and roots, to fuel Australian cookstoves.

Margaret and Henry Slaney became wonderful, emotionally supportive friends. They lived on a large, successful sheep station some distance from our camp. The first night I came as a visitor for dinner, I was scared nearly out of my wits while driving there in my jeep in late twilight. On leaving the highway and entering the drive leading to their home, I passed through a small woodland. Suddenly there came a loud, shrieking, menacing laugh. I jumped a foot. *What if some hoodlum is lurking there to kill me?* I thought in my sudden panic. On my telling the Slaneys of my terrifying experience, they laughed 'til tears ran down their faces. It was a kookaburra, a bird about the size of a small grouse and with a huge beak similar in shape but smaller than that of a South American toucan. When startled, it shrieks out this terrible loud, terrifying laugh. I remember my high school days when we sang a song about the kookaburra in the Glee Club. None of us, not even the music teacher, knew anything whatsoever about a kookaburra, but the song had a rollicking melody and we sang it several times a week. It went like this:

Kookaburra lives in the old gum treeee
Merry, merry king of the Bush is heeee
Laugh, kookaburra, laugh. . . .

Never in my wildest dreams had I ever thought I would meet with one and that it would scare me half to death.

The Slaney sheep station was a dramatic contrast to the marginal one that I had visited as an overnight guest. The couple evidently had had enough money to procure a huge tract of land, large enough to support a going operation, the knowledge and skill to make it a success, and the personal taste and resources to provide a pleasant home ambiance.

The house, built in traditional ranch style, was large enough and well enough finished in its interior to provide a most comfortable and pleasant setting. Nottingham lace curtains, some beautiful pictures, period mahogany furniture, and comfortable, attractive seating made a delightful living room. A large fireplace for chilly winter days was the center of architectural interest, and a large alcove housed mahogany dining furniture. All meals were eaten not at the kitchen table, but in that lovely dining room setting, complete with good china and silver and even linen napkins.

The Slaney kitchen was a classic example of standard kitchens throughout the land. The cooking was done on a shiny black cast-iron cookstove placed in a alcove with a window high on its wall to let heat escape. A Welsh cupboard stood against a wall, as always quaint and attractive and a clever, hardworking piece of kitchen furniture. Its bottom half consisted of a closed cupboard with two doors and a drawer above them. The family's silver and other cutlery were kept in the drawer, and on the shelves of the cupboard below were all the kitchen cooking utensils. Open shelves, usually three of them, were attached above the cupboard and held all of the china. Plates were stood on edge and overlapped, leaning against a back rail or a backing of solid wood. Cups hung from hooks on the undersides of the shelves. A table with some chairs completed the kitchen furnishings. The Slaneys and many of the more well-to-do families had additional cabinets built along other walls.

The exterior of the entire house was surrounded by a roofed porch. Chairs on all sides of this porch gave people a chance to always sit in the shade, all you had to do was move to the proper side of the house. You might even be lucky enough to also catch a few gentle breezes on a hot day. An ingenious water cooler hung from a rafter of every porch in the Australian countryside. This was a sheared sheepskin with legs clamped tightly together, and a clamp on the bottom which is the head end and which acted as the spigot. Water poured into this remarkable contraption evaporates slowly through the skin and thus cools to drinking temperature. If you ever get a chance, see the video *A Town like Alice,* which has you living for a couple of hours the typical life of Australians in the Bush and the Outback, complete with this water cooler and the "Darwin wave." I was astonished to see this Darwin wave on film years after coming back home because I had waved it hundreds of thousands of times in the Northern Territory, the Never Never Land, where flies are such a pest that one has to constantly keep slowly waving one hand in front of the face to keep them away.

Another video vividly depicting life in Australia is *The Sundowners,* a story of the life of an itinerant sheepshearer and his wife and child on their constant movement from station to station. Find it if you can. You'll love it.

Margaret Slaney was a gifted cook and made delicious meals, Australian style. The standard Sunday dinner entrée throughout Australia was a "joint," which meant a large roast of beef, lamb, veal, or occasionally mutton. Margaret could make a roast of mutton, spurned by many, taste like manna from Heaven. The joint was intentionally a large one; its second day consisted of cold slices, and on its third day it appeared as small pieces of meat in some kind of a seasoned gravy over rice or some other carbohydrate, often served as a delectable curry. Chicken was served occasionally as a relief from the usual red meat.

Margaret's "sponges" were a treat. It took me only one delightful bite to know what a "sponge" is. It's a sponge cake, perhaps the most popular dessert throughout the country at that time. This wonderful dessert came to the table as two standard cake layers with a spread of tart, sweet lemon curd between them and often topped with an artistic sprinkling of powdered sugar accomplished by sprinkling powdered sugar through a lacework doily. Margaret also introduced me to that most delightful of classic English desserts, the trifle. She said it was a good way to use up leftover sponge, and it is understandable that there would be plenty of it, for a sponge was the ubiquitous dessert offering throughout the whole country. The trifle bowl is made of a transparent glass of large diameter with straight six-inch sides resting on an attached pedestal, and a layer of sponge coats the bottom of the bowl. A tasty sweet wine is sprinkled on this layer of sponge, followed by a generous layer of delicious vanilla pudding, the traditional English custard, and then a thin layer of some favorite fruit marmalade or jelly. These layers are repeated in sequence until the bowl is filled. It is topped off with any decorative idea that comes to mind, often whipped cream with strawberries or other fruit dotting the top. Are you drooling? I am! I sometimes make it as the crown of a special holiday banquet and think lovingly of dear Margaret.

The Slaneys were exceptionally skillful at raising sheep. Henry showed me a steamer trunk full of blue, red, and gold prize ribbons he had won in livestock expositions with his silken-haired Spanish Merinos. When I first visited the Slaneys, it was breeding time and, with blushing cheeks, Margaret filled me in on the techniques of this operation. The flock had been shepherded into yards which served as holding pens. Many large wooden cages had been brought out for use. Margaret could hardly get the words out, she was so embarrassed, but she told me that first the ewes had all been sheared in a radius of about six inches around the vaginal entrance to facilitate breeding and that back in the early life of the lambs their long, wide tails had been cropped short for the same reason. The ewes presented a grotesque sight standing around with their naked backsides. Now at breeding time, and she chocked out the words, a young, active ram was selected and put into each cage. Also put into each cage were five or six ewes, and they were kept there all night. You can imagine the orgy! Have you ever seen a ram and noticed his testicles? They hang as a disproportionately large, heavy bag between his hind legs, and no one could doubt his ability to carry out his appointed task in the cage. The sheep are released from their cages the next morning into their expanse of grassland, mission accomplished, and the cages are refilled with more candidates each night.

The Slaneys did a little subsistence gardening. They raised a few chickens, which Margaret called her chooks, for whatever eggs the family would use and for an occasional chicken dinner. They raised a few vegetables near the house and, of course, some flowers.

Margaret kept sprigs of lavender between folded sheets in her linen press. This was a shelved cabinet in which she stored her linens, and before the advent of wardrobes in which to hang clothing there was also the clothes press for clothing. This was the custom throughout England and the Australian continent. In Australia, it never ceased to surprise me that clothes' closets were so rare as to be virtually nonexistent. Instead, there would be a tall, commodious, and often exquisitely beautiful wardrobe standing in nearly every bedroom, a true relic of the Victorian era.

Also, incidentally, I never ceased to wonder at the ingenious bedroom arrangement for a toilet: a potty chair for grown-ups. This was a roomy chair, often decoratively carved in Chippendale style, with an elaborately carved apron which concealed its lower container. At first sight one would think of it as a handsome armchair; then one would realize that the seat was a hinged lid. I have seen these wondrous inventions in antique shops in the years that followed, adapted into drawing room seating of great beauty, minus the inner works, of course.

The Slaneys, like all Australian country families, kept a cow or two, usually a Jersey, for providing the milk and cream the family needed. The Jersey cows were chosen because their rich milk provided more cream than does the milk of other breeds. In fact, the Jersey cream was so thick one couldn't even pour it. It was ladled out of containers with a spoon. Margaret, of Scottish heritage, told a story about a Scottish family who entertained their minister, a very strict Scotch Presbyterian, one evening in their home. They knew there was no use offering this teetotaler a highball, but to loosen up the conversation they came up with the novel idea of offering all a glass of milk, which was graciously accepted. What he didn't know was that in pouring a drink for everyone in the room the host had laced each glassful with a shot of liquor. The evening was a jovial success, and as the minister prepared to leave, his host asked if there was anything they could do for him. He answered, "Nothing I can think of just now, but when brrreeding time arrives, I'd surrrely like a calf from that coo."

In her Scottish way, Margaret referred to young people as "bonza laddies and lassies." They had three of them, two boys and a girl. The older boy and the girl were both in their teens and away at boarding school, and the sweet, timid seven-year old, Ralph, whose name they pronounced "Rafe," was living with his parents at home. Margaret explained what was obvious, that in the vast expanses of rural Australia a school near enough to walk or ride to was out of the question, so children were sent to boarding schools at a very tender age. They had brought Ralph to one, but the poor boy was so young he couldn't adapt to being away from home and he cried all the time. They brought him back, and his mother was teaching him with materials furnished by the government. Lessons were mailed back to a central education office to be corrected and returned with helpful suggestions. It appeared to be a very successful solution to an extremely difficult national problem. I noticed elsewhere, in less isolated areas, that children would often solve the distance problem by riding to school and back on their favorite pony. Some would stand on corners waiting to be picked up by a neighbor bringing his own children to school in his auto. What do you think these little girls were doing as they stood waiting? They were knitting stockings, et cetera, even little girls of nine or ten years of age.

I asked Margaret how Christmas was celebrated Down Under, as the seasons seemed so very topsy-turvey to me. She showed me some Australian Christmas cards, none of which displayed our familiar quaint New England towns with their small white churches and their charming steeples, nor was there a single card with a picture of a bundled-up couple riding through the snow in a horse-drawn cutter. For you poor dears reading this book who were born and reared in the auto age, riding in a cutter is the same as riding in a horse-and-buggy except that the buggy has no wheels but slides along in the snow on sleighlike runners. Instead of these quaint winter scenes, the Australian Christmas cards showed colored photographs of woodland scenes of Bush or a beach with swimmers or other visualizations depicting a midsummer holiday. Christmas dinner throughout all of Australia had to be built around a magnificent roast turkey, sometimes transported to an outdoor location for a picnic. Outdoor games followed unless everyone had to hurriedly answer an alert to fight brush fires, common in the depth of summer heat.

One evening dear Henry greeted me with a wail close to despair. "Me woife's crrrook! She thinks she's goin' to win tha warrr single-'anded!" He was speaking of her all-consuming volunteer war work. This sad wail telling me she was ill turned out to be prophetic, for at another assignment a year later I received the saddest, most despairing telegram. It told me that our wonderful, darling, sainted Margaret had undergone a drastic operation for cancer. As cancer treatment at that time was not as far advanced or as successful as it is now, of course this meant doomsday. I have cherished her memory and mourned her ever since.

How Can a Mere Woman Become an Honorary Marine?

From the very beginning of the American presence, Australian families expressed their gratitude to the American troops, their saviors, in many beautiful ways. One was by inviting the officers of a regiment to an evening's dancing party. The very night I arrived at Camp Balcombe, the officers of the Fifth Regiment brought me with them to one of these dances. On arrival, I was greeted by the hostess with the exclamation, "Oi'm amized at you jolly Amerrricans. You 'ave such beau-tiful teeth!" and she tapped my upper front incisors and asked, "Arr thay real?" I assured her that, yes, they were real. She explained, "Our soil 'ere in Ostr-eye-lia must be missin' some imporrrtant element, because nearrrly everrryone wearrrs denturrres at an astonishingly earrrrly eye-ge."

The homes in which these dances took place were elegant and spacious and included a room large enough to be used as a dance hall. I acquired a partner and we joined the dancers enthusiastically, but we were not aware that the highly waxed floor was so slippery that slow, cautious steps were necessary in order to stay upright. I soon slipped and fell to the floor, right on my backside. As I stood up and rubbed my derriere, I passed it off with the remark, "Wow! I surely fell on my keester that time." At this, all the young ladies hid their faces and scurried out of the room. I ambled out to join them and asked what horrible thing had I said? One young woman gave me my first lesson in Australian slang: "Wot we call ourr keester is whot you jolly Amerrricans call yourrr pussy!" The moral of this story is: BEWARE OF USING AMERICAN SLANG IN A STRANGE COUNTRY. It will very likely get you in Dutch!

The only insult I received in all my three years in Australia came at another of these dances. The host came up to me and said, "We didn't expect a camp follower. We had them in the First War, too!"

I was shocked, but regaining my composure, I explained that my duty was to provide recreational activities to combat troops on remote and isolated bases where an alarming incidence of deep chronic depression was occurring, making it necessary to bring the sufferers back to the States for long-term treatment in psychiatric hospitals, that this service was requested of the American Red Cross by the military, and that the first such request had come from the Aleutian Islands.

He laughed in scornful ridicule, "That's a neat excuse!"

His daughter then chimed in, "I'm naming my cat Tillie," the dreaded nickname which I thought I had left behind but which had followed me because someone had written me a letter addressed to "Miss Tillie Jones" with my APO (Army Post Office) number. I had been given the nickname Tillie the Toiler because I resembled Tillie Jones, the central figure in a popular comic strip of that name. She was a hardworking and often frustrated employee in a one-girl office.

Lieutenant Rust, fortunately, was standing nearby and heard me being accused of being nothing but a tart and he spoke up. "Tillie, you don't have to be subjected to abuse. We're taking you home right now, and a whole carful of us is going with you." He said, "I have never heard of a scurrilous attack like this in all my life." They brought me to my "digs," where we finished the evening in a delightful impromptu party of our own.

The Fifth Regiment Mess became as close as I could come to a home, right from the start. Since I was scheduled to take most of my meals there, the invitation included participation in the happy hour before the evening mess call. It was here that I worked at doing what I could for the morale of these wonderful men who were so good to me and who never even uttered the f——word. I worked at becoming a friend to each and every one of them. I already knew some of them, those who had extended themselves in kindnesses to me. One was Walter Goodman, a very pleasant, handsome, black-haired young lawyer from Chicago. Others were Lieutenant Rust, a stalwart friend, Charles Baker, one of the kindest and dearest men in the world, and various others. The two chaplains had been our buddies from the very beginning: the Catholic chaplain, friendly but somewhat austere, and the very easy to know Protestant chaplain, Ansgar Sovik, a Norwegian from Minneapolis. Throughout all my seven months with the Marines, the two chaplains, Neil Bennett, and I were a team, practically one office. We referred matters back and forth between our offices so often that a person could hardly tell one of us from another.

In my efforts at getting to know these men, I developed a plan for building a new friendship with three officers every evening. I engaged each of my new acquaintances in conversation, getting his exact name, hometown, description of his family, life experiences, and interests and making careful mental notes of distinguishing physical features. Immediately upon leaving the mess hall, I wrote it all down in a handy notebook, including a physical description, leaving extra lines in case more information might be added. Before mess each day, I studied and memorized those notes. On arriving at mess, I sought out these new friends, called them by name, and asked some friendly personal question like, "How are things in Sioux Falls?," then added three more new friends to my list in the same way. This gave me twenty-one friends per week, eighty-six each month, and before very long I was a personal friend of every one of those officers. They marveled at this accomplishment and spoke of it as a triumph of virtual superhuman intelligence. I never told them that I had learned, early on, the riddle about how to get to Carnegie Hall: PRACTICE!! My effort at making friends was greatly appreciated. Colonel John thanked me and said I was the only person who knew the names of all the officers in the regiment.

The officers took me into their collective bosom. They staged a mock ceremony in which they declared me officially an "Honorary Marine" and bestowed upon me the right to wear their gift of their *forr a-jierre*. The *forr a-jierre* is a high military decoration awarded by the French government to the Fifth Regiment in a strategic battle of World War I at, I think, Château-Thierry and Belleau Wood. The *forr a-jierre* is a circle of a braided strip of scarlet and green yarns with short tasseled ends extending from it. The honored serviceman slips his arm through it and fastens it to his shoulder with his epaulet strap. I wore it proudly everywhere.

The officers also gave me much later on, as a lasting memento, a small silver tray with the inscription: "From the Fifth Regiment, First Marine Division to Miss Tillie Jones, Honorary Marine," followed by the date. On this tray rested two fluted silver containers to hold, surprisingly now but at that time very important, cigarettes on the coffee table. It is hard for us now to realize how universally pervasive at that time was the habit of smoking. Everybody smoked; it was the thing to do. Men in the military in both World Wars I and II, under unbearable stresses, smoked virtually all the time.

The happy hour at the mess never began until "the sun was over the yardarm," but in order to explain that this is only a general term, our wonderful Colonel John explained to me that "the sun is always over the yardarm somewhere." Happy hour always began with a highball at the bar. I was not a drinker, but was I going to be prissy and refuse? No, I couldn't, so I'd have one drink with them, sometimes possibly two. What I didn't know was that these dear men had secretly laid bets on how many drinks I could down without getting plastered, as they had laced every highball with a double shot of liquor. Fortunately, I never collapsed, but I have always been glad that a hearty meal followed immediately thereafter. I wish they had not played that game, but I know that to them it was only harmless fun.

On December 7, 1942, the officers of the Fifth Regiment gave a wonderful dinner dance in Melbourne to express appreciation to the families who had so graciously entertained them during their stay at Camp Balcombe. Printed invitations, formal dress, an elegant orchestra, all the trimmings! The date was chosen as the anniversary of the bombing of Pearl Harbor. The Tractor Company gave me my evening gown and wrap. In those times of severe shortages of consumer goods, I was lucky to find in a Melbourne shop my beautiful ball gown of full-skirted cream-colored taffeta with a sleeveless, close-fitting bodice supported by three-inch-wide bright, deep green shoulder straps. A similarly wide band of deep green surrounded the upper edge of the bodice. I was fortunate, too, to find an elegant floor-length, puffed-sleeved black velvet wrap.

One of the dearest men whoever lived asked to be my escort; he was Charlie Baker, who had been a Marine guard on the battleship *Arizona* at Pearl Harbor and had written an account of that fateful morning. A few weeks after the party he gave his written story to me because he was going to leave on a solitary mission and could take nothing with him except for the bare essentials of living. He told me that if he survived he would look me up and ask for it back and asked me to promise that if I did not hear from him I would have it published. I promised, but woe is me, although I never heard from him again, his account has been lost somehow (possibly stolen?), and no matter how I hunt, I have never been able to find it. It is one of the greatest regrets of my life.

Back at the party, it was wonderful to see what a thrilling event it was and what a marvelous time everyone had. At one pont in the festivities, however, I was approached by the parents of a young Australian girl who asked me in worried tones why their daughter, in all of those months, did not have a steady American boyfriend. I told them, "Be thankful she didn't. These relationships were all romantically and emotionally intense, extremely intense. How would you, as parents, feel on observing your brokenhearted daughter after the object of her affections leaves to go into battle and, very likely, never returns? Also, how would returning Australian servicemen view the scene when they came back and realized that there is probably only one girl in a hundred who had not been the intimate companion of an American serviceman?" This seemed to comfort them, and they walked away visibly relieved.

In fact, these romantic liaisons were perhaps the most striking and pervasive feature of military life in areas with a civilian population. This was especially understandable among the Marines in the Melbourne and Mornington area, who lived every hour of the day with the terrible realization that their life on this earth was almost certain to be horribly terminated in the very near future. This realization and the need to cope with it not only dominated the thoughts of the troops; it also pervaded the administrative departments of the Marine Corps. There was, for instance, a regulation that no one could marry without permission from his commanding officer, and this permission was almost never given. One of the officers read to me his response to a request to marry which he denied "because of the extreme and intense danger which lies before him." Then the officer told me that those seemingly harsh words put the hazard in too gentle terms, but he hadn't the heart to tell it like it was. However, some very few marriages were permitted, and one could only surmise that those were cases in which a baby was on the way. Even those required a written report of investigation of the prospective bride provided by the American Red Cross. Although these interviews with the young woman and her parents were normally conducted by the field director or assistant field director, I was occasionally asked to perform this service and I submitted the customary half-page report of observable family surroundings and a cursory description of the young woman.

The Australian girls were overwhelmed by the charming consideration the American men gave them. The general attitude of Australian men toward women was very hard for me to understand. A woman existed for the purpose of grocery shopping, meal preparation, dish washing, doing the laundry, cleaning the house, caring for the children, tending the garden, and being a bed partner, one-two-three-thank-you-ma'am. Recreation, to a man, meant sitting at a bar with the fellows, drinking and swapping stories, man-talk, and outdoor sports. They had no idea whatever of social companionship with their women, and as for gentlemanly habits, forget it! These downtrodden women had risen up en masse on one issue, however, and had gotten legislation pushed through that closed the bars during mealtime. My amazement at the Australian men's attitude toward women was finally made understandable in a book about Australia I read last year written by one of them, an Aussie himself. The settlement of the continent began in 1810, with the landing of a shipload of English convicts docking at the beautiful harbor of Sydney, which became the first city of Australia. Prior to our Revolutionary War, England had used Maryland and Georgia as prison labor sites, where the convicts worked out the terms of their sentences and were released as civilians at the termination of their prison terms. With the Revolutionary War, England lost this convenient dumping ground, and until 1810 she housed her convicts in rotting hulks anchored around London. Disease, depravity, and escape caused such a furor that a different solution for housing them had to be found. Australia had been circumnavigated by Captain Cook in 1788 and claimed as an English possession. It proved a heaven-sent alternative. These shipments of convicts sent to work out their sentences in Australia continued until 1868, and prison encampments proliferated along the east coast and southward into Tasmania. The early construction of buildings, roads, and other necessary accommodations was the result of convict labor. After the prison sentences had been completed, these former convicts were released into the harsh, wild countryside to fend for themselves, a bleak prospect. Any who murdered another human being were summarily executed.

Many more men than women convicts were brought to Australia; fifty-two thousand men, but only two hundred fifty women, most of them prostitutes, were brought there. The society that developed was definitely male-oriented. One of the most available jobs for the released convicts was the loading and unloading of commercial vessels in the brisk trade with China involving alcohol products, and a great deal of pervasive drunkenness developed. A corollary to this historical account emerges. Since virtually all Australians are descendants of convicts, a sense of shame was discernible even when I was there, and on some occasions one of them would proudly explain to me that his parents or grandparents had come to the new country as free men. Most who came of their own free will were businessmen, and there were some few others in the professions as well. Imagine the delight of the young Australian girls at meeting American servicemen who opened doors for them, helped them on with their coats, chatted with their parents, went shopping with them, helped with the dishes, and, above all, enjoyed spending social time with them. What a treat! They were being treated like ladies, and they loved it.

The American servicemen, however, were faced with something different—mortal urgency. If you know that very soon your young life will, almost certainly, abruptly and tragically end, how do you view the days you have left? You are driven to live, and live fully while you have that precious time. This led to the extreme intensity, the urgency, in these romantic affairs.

Of course sex was a part of it. How could it not be? Those who could "shacked up" with their temporary, but extremely dear, loved ones. Some officers, too, shacked up as well. One, in all kindliness and solicitude, asked me, "Why don't you shack up, too, Tillie?" Could I hurt his feelings by telling him such a question was unacceptable? Of course not, so after a moment's thought I lightly replied, "Because I'm in love with all of you. How could I possibly choose one? Besides, how could I ever find the time?"

Coming Events Cast Their Shadow before Them

Melbourne, what a lovely city! My visits there were all too few, mostly only the monthly trip to drop off my written report of the past month's work. I always gave myself the treat of a leisurely ramble through its streets, enjoying the beauty of its stately Victorian mansions surrounded by their spacious lawns, which weren't lawns at all, but magnificent flower gardens. The whole city had a Victorian air, even keeping some of the old Victorian customs, it was just my cup of tea. Situated down in the southeast corner of the continent, it enjoyed the added blessing of a Mediterranean type of climate, similar to that of Los Angeles, and its inhabitants were spared the struggle of constantly coping with the tropical heat which intensified as one went farther and farther northward. Altogether a delightful place to live.

The euphoria of enjoyment I had looked forward to in what turned out to be my last trip to the city became mixed with puzzlement and some uncertainty. When I walked into our Red Cross office and laid my monthly report on the desk of our field director, Wayne Clark, his secretary, Mrs. Smith, motioned me over to the far side of the room. In a very low voice she said, "Oi'm so glad to see you, Tillie. Oi've been witing [waiting] for you to come. Oi need to ask your advoice." At this she looked nervously at Wayne Clark and edged me farther still away from him as he sat at his desk. "Oi've been offered a position in Brisbane and Oi know it's pretty far north. You get a much better screw. Should Oi go? 'Twill be good for me daughter, too. She's just ite-een [eighteen]. Should Oi go? 'Tis the cloimate (climate), don't you know."

I was dumbfounded. Virtually every American knows what a screw is and is usually too polite to talk about it. Yet here was this middle-aged, matronly woman willing to pull up stakes and move from this beautifully benign climate to the oppressive heat of the tropics in order to have a better screw. Many thoughts raced through my mind. Did Wayne Clark have anything to do with it? I had always thought of him as a gentleman; one of the good guys. And what does climate have to do with the quality of a screw? Is there something, to say the least, unusual about the Australians? But a stranger in a strange land does not make waves, and I couldn't run the risk of creating a social debacle by asking this woman, whom I hardly knew, about a screw. So I extricated myself from the situation, bowing out answering, "Oh, Mrs. Smith. I'm so new to this country and I've had very little contact with the Australian people because I'm at the American Marine Corps camp almost all of the time. I know so little about Australian life that I couldn't possibly advise you toward any decision. You know I'd help if I could." She sighed and I patted her on the shoulder and left. (But a screw? What's a screw got to do with it, anyway? An Australian puzzle.)

Training at both Camp Balcombe and Mount Martha was reaching a high point of perfection. Men marched in their drills in perfect, intricate precision. Practice of amphibious landings had become an easy routine. Men began telling me about their longest training march ever, in which they were going to hike fifty miles carrying backpacks weighing thirty pounds or more and sleeping overnight on open land. They spoke of it as a challenge, confident that they were up to it. The hospital had been losing its patients and now stood virtually empty, its malaria-stricken population now fully recovered and back in training.

There was an overall atmosphere of intensified activity and a hint of things to come. Men began saying that they thought the Marines would soon be moving out. Everywhere there was a sense of urgency.

The Aussies talked, too, of the Marines' moving out much more openly than did the men themselves. They seemed to know more about military matters than we did. One night my cleaning lady saw my light being switched on as I returned home to sleep and she came over "just for a chat, don't you know." We talked pleasantly for a time about our homes and our lives. She told me about some "R.C.s" (Roman Catholics) she had met and remarked that they probably would make good friends after all. This last remark was typical of the prevailing attitude among the Australian populace, that anyone who was not exactly like them was "an outsider." People looked askance at Catholics, Jews, and Orientals. A lady once told me she was so thankful that we Yanks had come because, being of Irish descent, she never really had "belonged" and we Americans, with our attitude of accepting everybody, had changed her life and much of the social atmosphere about her. Insularity can cause an ingrown attitude in people, and the American presence was a breath of fresh air.

My cleaning lady then began telling some of her favorite jokes. One has stuck with me to this day, although I have never told it to a soul. She began, "A Scotsman wearing kilts was buying vegetables at an open-air fresh produce market. He told a woman at one of the stands that he would like to buy a head of cabbage. Many Scotsmen wore no underwear under their kilts, and he had gathered up the front of his skirt to hold his previous purchases, giving the viewer a free show. She was insulted and shouted at him, 'Go get your cabbage were you got your carrot and spinach!' " We had a good laugh and she departed with only the usual "ta-ta," equivalent to our "so long." I realized later that her visit had been an intentional farewell and that she, my cleaning lady, knew more about military affairs than I did.

I had been honored a week or two before this by personal visits of two esteemed generals. The first visitor was General Krueger, Commander, as I remember, of the Sixth Army. He ostensibly came for just a little chat, but no busy general drops in to see a little Red Cross lady just for a chat. I still don't know why he came except perhaps to size up the general situation. He was a charming, kindly, old-shoe type of man, and it was a delightful visit. He told me he was a maverick, but he looked like no maverick to me because a maverick is a misfit in a herd of cattle. He explained that a maverick, however, in the Army is a person who reaches officer status not by attending West Point, but by rising up through the ranks. Knowing how many steps and how many vicissitudes one experiences in that process, one wonders that anyone ever makes it. I did figure out, though, the reason for his visiting our camp, which he surely did not do as just a pleasure jaunt. He was planning and coordinating the move-out.

A day or so after General Krueger's visit, in walked Gen. Lemuel Shepherd, Commandant of the entire Marine Corps. He, too, was planning the move-out. I shall never know the real reason for this visit to me, but I think it was out of the kindness of his heart, for this kindly, friendly, relaxed man, who had the inner strength of a warrior, gave me one of the most important and cherished lessons of my life. After talking pleasantly for a few minutes, he looked into my eyes and said, "Tillie, would you like me to tell you what I have learned about how to take war?"

I answered, "Yes, please do," and this is what he said: "When someone comes to you, as eventually it is bound to happen, and tells you that various people have died in battle, you are going to have to receive the news with regret, but you're also going to have to not let it devastate you, and then you are going to have to go on with your work. If you don't, you will be so overwhelmed by grief that you won't be able to function, and you thereby become, yourself, a casualty. You're going to have to be able to say, and mean it, 'Oh, what a shame. Ping-Pong anyone?'" His words rang through my mind every day of the coming years, and they gave me the strength to tough it out. I did have some temporary slipups, it's true, but I could slip right back into his groove, and this saved me.

The days following the farewell visit from my cleaning lady were days of an increasingly taut atmosphere throughout the camp, and in this prevailing air of tension people are liable to let slip some inadvertent word or gesture which reveals military secrets they never intended to divulge. They may not have been aware that they were giving the game away at all. In fact, one morning some days after my cleaning lady's visit, a rather high-ranking Fifth Regiment officer came into our office and hurriedly asked me to phone an Australian family to cancel their plans to entertain him in an overnight visit the coming weekend. I told him I would be happy to make the phone call, and then it happened; I inadvertently used two words, harmless in civilian parlance but technical in the military. To us in the civilian life "stand by" means to relax and be willing to continue the spoken-of activity at some undetermined later date. However, the military meaning of "stand by" is to stand at rigid attention awaiting immediate further orders. I told him I would relay his message to the Australian family and that I would ask them to stand by. In a knee-jerk reaction, without taking time to think, he blurted out, "Oh, no! Just tell them to cancel," and he hurried out.

I knew, then and there, that I had gotten the word, the official word: The Marines were moving out before that very weekend. That night I packed my luggage, and it is well that I did, for when I arrived at our office the next morning, there on the desk lay a written order terminating my assignment with the Marines. I immediately turned in my precious jeep, and a driver took me to my little half-house, where he helped me out with my two footlockers. I stood there on the walk in full regalia. My coat was flung over my shoulder; in one hand I grasped my handbag and overnight case, and in the other, my metal helmet and mess kit. What, no guitar? No guitar. It wasn't there on my back this time. A Marine had begged me piteously to allow him to buy it from me. I hadn't the heart to refuse him, so I had given it to him. The mouth organ had suffered the same fate.

As I waited for my ride to the transport depot, I reflected on the lesson I had learned so many times before and which I am sure the Australian girls would now learn the hard way: in war, everything, yes, everything, is temporary.

C'est le guerre!

The sequel to this story of the incomparable and heroic men of the Fifth and Seventh Marine Regiments came to pass over a year later as I stood one day on a street corner in Brisbane. A well-modulated masculine voice behind me called out, "Hello, Tillie!"

I turned and saw, to my great surprise, one of the officers of the Fifth Regiment. I had had no news of them in all that time, and I asked urgently, "Where did you go? What happened?"

He told me, "We took the island of Peleliu, but oh, at what a cost! The whole First Marine Division made the landing."

I hardly dared ask it, but I choked out the words, "Were there many casualties?"

His answer was, "it was a slaughter."

I asked anxiously if anyone had survived.

He said, "Almost nobody. In fact, I don't know why I am alive. It was pure chance. The only lucky ones were those wounded and still breathing, who were sent back to hospitals in the States."

I answered, "Oh, my God," but I held up fairly well. I then began asking about individuals and I asked about Walter Goodman, that nice young lawyer from Chicago. He answered, "We had just stepped onto the beach and I turned and saw Walter. He was flying up into the air in a thousand pieces."

This was too much for me and I burst into a torrent of tears. He put his arm around my shoulders to comfort me, but it didn't help. I walked away sobbing my heart out.

I had intended but had become unable to ask about various others, and about Charlie Baker, the dearest and kindest of all men, who had been my escort at the farewell dinner dance and who had told me good-bye, that he was leaving on a solitary mission. I knew in my heart then what that mission was. He was the one who had been sent ahead as an advance scout, dropped onto the island by parachute or helicopter to live in secret off the land and send back radio messages about terrain, enemy strength and locations, and other pertinent data. I know now that he must have been killed in this effort. How could he possibly have survived?

Have I ever tried to look anybody up? Are you kidding? My only visits are to the graveyard of my memories.

VII
Sights and Sounds of Sydney

While the Marines were moving out, I, too, was on the move back to Sydney again on layover to await my second assignment. On my first layover, Sydney, the largest and most metropolitan of all the cities of Australia, was an interesting place to be. It was also considered by all Australians as the very best place to be if one could possibly afford it. Considering the penal history of Australia, the people had developed somewhat of a risk-taking attitude toward life. They had a particular little saying when embarking on a chancy venture, that meant if they struck it rich, they'd live in Sydney, but if they lost, they'd have to live in the Bush. Thus the popular saying, "It's Sydney or the Bush for me."

On this visit, I enjoyed the cinema and the churches and was fortunate to attend a Gilbert and Sullivan operetta, *Ruddygore*, produced by the original company, the D'Oyly Carte. *Ruddy* is a takeoff on that forbidden word *bloody*. The objection to the use of the word *bloody* had to have arisen in England in order for a pair of English composers to have built an entire satirical musical comedy on the word. In Australia, one could use *goddamn, hell, God,* and *Jesus Christ* as epithets without causing a raised eyebrow, but you'd better not say *bloody.* Consequently, everyone said it all the time. It was bloody awful, bloody good, bloody bloke, bloody everything, and I became a little lonesome for those other old swear words.

At one point during my second stay in Sydney, I was befriended by three genial and very pleasant Australian Army officers who gave me a wonderful treat. Taking turns, one each day, they took me on guided tours of Sydney and its environs in an automobile with a driver, which freed them to give me pointers about the lovely city. After a few days, they were called to their new assignments, just as I expected to be called. I would like, in passing, to offer a suggestion to Australian Army planners. Consider advising your officers and enlisted men about two possible options regarding the very roomy short-legged trousers of their uniforms. The first option is be sure to wear briefs such as jockey shorts underneath them. The second option is if you don't wear underwear, just remember never to cross your legs, especially in the backseat of a motorcar, lest you embarrass your fellow passengers with a display of the family jewels. I could not say anything to these kindly hosts, so I suddenly developed an intense interest in the outdoor landscape. I did learn one thing though: if you've seen one, you've seen 'em all!

I enjoyed sampling the life of an explorer of Sydney's restaurants and lunch counters. The chefs were excellent cooks, although I could not bring myself to sample some of their most highly prized offerings. It seemed at the time that there was a preoccupation with variety meats such as creamed sweetbreads, creamed brains, and heart and kidney, and, of course, there was always liver. The liver I could eat, but the others I could not even bring myself to try. One evening at an elegant home in a different locale, I was served a piece of steak and kidney pie which my hostess had laboriously and lovingly prepared as a special treat. I could barely eat it but gave it my best college try and got it down. Steak and kidney pie was considered a prestigious entrée at the time and is apparently tedious to prepare. Of course, it was only me, I was simply not used to these gustatory adventures.

At various lunch counters many servicemen, particularly Americans, were devoted to a breakfast, lunch, and dinner offering of "stike 'n' eggs." Steak and eggs—imagine the combination! The servicemen though, Americans and Allies alike, gobbled it down and loved every morsel.

I noticed, however, that in my entire three years in Australia I was never offered one tiny slice of pork—not one. When one thinks about it, the reason becomes obvious. The soil is too poor in Australia to support the growing of corn, the chief food in hog raising, and imported pork was out of the question in those days of consumer scarcities.

During this stay in Sydney, I spent much of my time at the newest, largest, finest hotel in the country, the Australia Hotel. I enjoyed the meals, using the Red Cross–allotted per diem, the balance coming from my own pocket. I sat in the lobby along with other servicepeople from Australia, America, and other countries, who, like me, were awaiting transfer. These were very interesting conversations.

Not only were there servicepeople, but a large number of civilians, too, were constantly coming and going. It was here in the lobby and on the streets of Sydney that I happily continued my love affair with the "digger hat," used as standard topping in casual dress and in all of Australia as the standard work hat. Every man had one. The digger hat is a triumph of brown felt, with a creased crown and a rather wide brim jauntily turned up on one side. It is universally becoming. I don't know if everyone feels as I do about it, but I get the vibes that the digger hat says to every man that no matter how tough the go, there is always a brighter side.

One day, I was shocked to my very gizzard while walking alongside another Red Cross person. I was wearing my winter uniform, which I had had to have made in Australia because the Red Cross suppliers had an idea that all of Australia was always warm and it was patently out of the question to order one sent from the States. This winter uniform was needed because in the southern part of this country there are some stretches of quite cool weather, often for rather long periods, and there is almost no provision for indoor heating throughout the whole continent. You simply put on another sweater. Although there were all kinds of clever, inventive arrangements for coping with the heat, in the colder weather "you puts up with it and you takes your chances." So I, always chilly, had to have a winter uniform. When it came to my own good looks, however, the tailoring of my made-to-order winter uniform fell flat. It was not chic, it was far less than glamorous, to say the very least, and I always felt apologetic about my appearance when I wore it.

One day as I walked along a wall leading to the elegant suite of ladies' rooms, the Red Cross woman who was walking beside me continued toward the same destination. Glancing in her direction and sizing her up, I said to myself, *Who's that dumpy-looking frump? Some social worker from Chicago, I suppose.* As we walked along, she kept in step with me and she even turned her head toward me when I turned mine toward her. Finally I realized what was happening and said, "My God, it's me!" The entire wall was a mirror.

The elegant ladies' lounge room could seat many femmes who were waiting for someone, primping, or just relaxing, and there were always quite a few of us enjoying its features. As one woman walked through to the toilet room, she announced that she was going to "shed a tear for Nelson."

I said to the others, "Shed a tear for Nelson? Who's Nelson? What's he got to do with it?"

One of them answered, "It's a bit of a long story, but would you like to hear it?"

"Yes, yes indeed," and she proceeded: "Admiral Lord Nelson was one of England's greatest naval heroes. As a young man, he fell in love with his boss's beautiful young wife. This seemed a welcome arrangement for the elderly husband, and when he died Nelson lived with the lovely widow for years and finally married her. He was a man of great charisma. He saved the Empire leading the fleet in a crucial naval victory and was knighted. He lost an arm in the engagement. Later, he led the fleet to another decisive victory in the Mediterranean in which he lost his life. Throughout his entire naval career, he was the romantic idol of every woman, both young and old, in England. When he died the women all wept oceans of tears and ever since, when a lady walks toward the toilet, she is likely to mention that she is going to shed a tear for Nelson."

There is hardly a woman who is satisfied with her weight. One day, a young lady entered the ladies' lounge, stepped onto the scales which stood in the lounge, carefully weighed herself, and sighed, "Oh deah, ite stone six."

I said to her, "A stone is fourteen pounds, which means you weigh eight times fourteen plus six, or 112 pounds plus six, adding up to 118 pounds. Why don't you just throw away the stone and tell yourself that you weight 118 pounds? It's so much simpler."

I quickly discovered I had pressed her worry button, for, visibly shaken, she said, "That would never do. 'Ow would Oi ever know 'ow many stone Oi wye?" Well, you can't win 'em all.

All things come to pass in their own good time, and in its own good time I received my orders to report to a transport unit to join five other Red Cross women en route to another assignment.

VIII

Eagles and Airplanes Both Have Wings

We boarded that tiny one-engine plane with an explorer's feeling of stepping into the unknown. There was Hertha, a hospital recreation worker; Nancy, a club recreation worker; Flora, another club recreation worker; a secretary; a social worker; and yours truly; plus the pilot. There was also our luggage, including my special extra footlocker, which I had had to use all my powers of persuasion to once again get aboard, and there were also wax paper sacks just in case one had the erps. We were told we were to complete the Red Cross unit in a remote Army post in the Northern Territory. I suppose that is all they dared tell us at the time because our destination was in an area called the Never Never Land.

Who would ever have thought that this sweet little central Wisconsin farm girl would ever be flying across an entire continent including one of the three greatest deserts in the world, to the far edge of nowhere, and who would ever have dreamed that she would be airsick and vomit all the way, and who would have ever doubted that through it all she would tough it out? Nobody, but nobody.

Our plane rose into the air and we flew over the coastal area near Sydney, over a low part of the Great Dividing Range, over the Bush, which is an uncrowded woodland containing eucalyptus trees and bushy plants and dotted here and there with billabongs. A billabong is a small pond fed by groundwater welling up through a crevice in the underlying rock layer. The Bush gave way to the Outback, an area of smaller and smaller eucalyptus trees farther and farther apart, with fewer and fewer bits of vegetation, then over the Far Outback, which is the same thing as the Outback but with even smaller and more scattered vegetation, finally giving way to the Great Desert of Australia.

I had never contemplated a visit to the Outback, with the wartime restrictions and the ban on personal travel, but as we know too well, war brings many surprises. One of these was an unplanned visit there. An eagle had flown into a wing of our plane, which we had to have repaired before we could fly on. We put down at one of the tiniest settlements in the world, aptly named Longreach. Long reach is right! If a person would think of making a living in the Outback, it would just about have to be as a sheep or cattle station owner with vast acreage comprising many square miles, because the sparse vegetation of this dryer area could not support the standard number of sheep or cattle per square mile. Consequently, distances between homesteads were great, each one being many, many miles from its nearest neighbor.

Realizing these problems of distance, it follows that journeys to lay in basic supplies or to transact business would be long and likely to require an overnight layover, making it necessary to provide a small hotel at the intersection of the trail-like roads, and small, very small, settlements grew up around them.

Such a settlement was Longreach, made up of a small family-run hotel, a general store stocking only basics, a filling station, a few minimal houses, and that was all. Of course, one could land a plane anywhere in those flat, open spaces.

Our hotel accommodations were minimal but adequate, and our hosts were helpful and gracious. The hotel seemed typical of many other widely scattered accommodations throughout the Outback and the Bush.

As we six Red Cross women and our pilot sat in the dining room at the evening meal ("tea," remember), we were greeted by another diner, a sheep station owner also on a one-night stay. We had an interesting conversation for a half hour or so, and then he turned to me and said, "Oi wish you'd come with me on a visit to me family. Oi'd loik you to meet me son. 'E would loik to be married." Taken by surprise, I still remembered to be gracious and replied that in any other circumstances I'd feel fortunate to accept his kind invitation, but I was committed to this war work and had to board the plane with the rest of our group as soon as it was ready, which I thought would be the next day.

The prospect, even in the imagination, of living in such isolation was unthinkable to me, and I wondered how these people could cope with it. What they did, those who could afford it, was spend several weeks, from time to time, in Sydney and every second year or so spend several months in Mother England. Since they were already halfway around the world, they would continue westward on a round-the-world tour. On talking with such travelers later, I asked what places they visited in the United States. They replied New York and either San Francisco or Los Angeles. Although their trains passed through Chicago, they didn't visit this city. I asked them why they didn't also stop and explore Chicago, the great metropolis of the Middle West. With an air of almost horror, they quickly replied that what with Al Capone and the other Chicago gangsters, they were afraid of Chicago and didn't dare step off the train.

As I contemplated those long visits to Sydney and to England as a part of a round-the-world tour which these isolated people of the Outback indulged in, I thought, "Nice work if you can get it. But what about those unlucky people who can't afford these trips and are stuck out there away from everything."

Our airplane wing repaired, we proceeded to fly over the Great Australian Desert to our destination in the Never Never Land. The desert is about the size and shape of the Sahara, the immense stretches of level desert land broken only by one special landscape feature: a large monolith of reddish brown stone called Ayres Rock in the direct center of the desert. It was a great experience to fly over it. Unfortunately, our route did not include flying over Alice Springs, the only town in central Australia, 275 miles from the Rock.

Thus we continued on our flight and I continued with my airsick vomiting until we reached our destination in the Never Never Land, a place most people do not know anything about, nor would they ever want to. Certainly, very few people know that it even exists. The Never Never Land, in the words of Australian friends, is "the land you never, never want to go to, and if you do go, you never, never want to go back."

IX

Adelaide River—Bear Every Hardship, Cope with Every Inconvenience, Graciously, and Don't Complain

We disembarked at an Army camp which was called Adelaide River because the Adelaide River was the only physical feature nearby with which it could be identified. There also was a tiny settlement about fourteen miles from this Army camp.

How does one describe that pothole, that back door of nature? Perhaps if we wanted to give it a descriptive name it could be called God's Lost Acres. How does one describe this camp, this hellhole of deprivations, of unspeakable food, of powdered eggs, of distrust and suspicion, of noncooperation, of unbearable heat, this place of personal sacrifices for everyone in it? These frustrations, sacrifices, and deprivations kept gnawing on all of us so much that everyone had a hard time keeping even-tempered. Still, I was sent there to work, and I got busy at it.

The camp itself was built along both sides of a wide, deep ravine. This ravine made the perfect divider between Officers' Country and Enlisted Men's Country. A narrow wooden footbridge spanned the ravine allowing single file access. The only buildings on the camp were two pavilions, one in Enlisted Men's Country and one in Officers' Country. These pavilions were interestingly built, well adapted to the deep tropics. The pavilions had a roof and the walls were only waist-high, leaving a generous open space between walls and roof which enabled us to catch every breeze. The officers' pavilion was used as a mess hall, with tables and chairs, and a kitchen was attached at the rear. The service was impeccable but the meals unspeakable, complete with powdered eggs every morning for breakfast. They were hideous. I forced myself to eat them because I knew I had to keep up my strength, but it took all my willpower. We subsisted the rest of the day on Army rations. If you are really searching for a way to do penance, try powdered eggs and Army rations.

The pavilion in Enlisted Men's Country was used as the dayroom, complete with tables and chairs. It was also their recreation spot.

How did those enlisted men eat? They lined up in single file, holding their metal mess kits, which were divided down the middle for either hot and cold or dry and wet food. As they stood in line, the Sergeant plopped some of those rations, that unspeakable food, into those mess kits. They stood, squatted, or went into the dayroom to sit at a table to eat. When they had finished, they had to come back to where they had got their food, and there stood a huge corrugated steel vat filled with boiling, and I mean boiling, hot soapy water. A very coarse-bristled brush hung by a chain from the vat, and, boy, you'd better scrub out that mess kit! They then had to dowse it in another vat of boiling, and I mean boiling, water for rinsing. Every man washed his mess kit in the same vat and rinsed it in the same vat. The Army had learned from bitter experience that these two vats, one of boiling soapy water and the other of vigorously boiling clear water, were absolutely necessary to prevent disease.

The enlisted men lived, as we did, in the ever-present pyramidal tents. Theirs stood in rows along the edge of the ravine, making "streets" which were only little paths between the rows of tents. The tents stretched for some distance and slept four men in each one. The officers slept only two in a tent; and we women, three in a tent.

One thing that absolutely astounded me was one of the greatest incongruities I have ever seen. In front of many enlisted men's tents stood a white wicker chaise lounge. One of the men explained that when Darwin, a hundred miles north of Adelaide River, was bombed on February 19, 1942, its people moved out en masse. The entire city was totally evacuated, and that was where the chaise lounges came from. Well, at least they had one item of comfort, a lovely means of relaxation.

The pyramidal tents of Officers' Country were lined up on the other side of the ravine. The ones closest to the pavilion contained the minimal administrative offices. Among them was a Red Cross office headed by a field director whom I shall call Walt. I wouldn't dream of mentioning his name. He was a real son of a sea cook, and

I'm too much of a lady for a more graphic description. He took the written reports that I prepared every month to be sent to Red Cross Channels, had the secretary retype them, and then signed his name to them as though he had written them himself. Who was I to do the work and then write about it? Oh no, he was the field director and those were his reports. My name was never included in any way. He knew nothing of building morale. The field directors, of course, simply *had* to be men. It seemed as though the only requirements were that they wore men's trousers and said they would be willing to go. I don't know any other criteria for choosing these Red Cross field director misfits. There were some few fine ones, however, the exceptions that proved the rule. I recently asked a friend who had been a Red Cross Recreation Club director in Europe if my opinion regarding the field directors was accurate. She replied that yes, it was, and that my foul impression of them was not just an aberration.

Walt had one helper, the secretary, who had flown over the Great Australian Desert with the rest of us. She was a lackluster but pleasant person. Everyone in the camp, officers, enlisted men, and Red Cross personnel, was living in a highly stressful environment. Perhaps the secretary was the wisest of us all, for she relieved her frustrations from time to time by getting drunk.

There was a little rise some distance back of the double row of officers' tents and here was established our women's enclave. It consisted of two tents for sleeping three each, a shower head outside in front of one of them, and in front of the other tent was a shelf nailed between two trees. An enameled granite washbasin rested on it, and beside it was a saucer for soap. Two galvanized metal pails accompanied this layout, one for fresh washing water, the other for the used wash water. For our further convenience, a two-holer privy had been built quite some distance from our tents. It had to be far enough back so that no unpleasant aroma would be wafted in our direction, and in intense heat this was a distinct possibility that had to be dealt with.

Three narrow bunk beds had been placed in each tent. Each bed had a scaffolding of metal framework rising from the corners of the bed, and from it hung a mosquito net. This mosquito net was standard equipment in many Australian homes. You had to use it here because the insects and other pests were really amazing.

Mosquitoes swarmed about in such large numbers that at night you could hear them buzz like the obligato on the violins of a symphony orchestra. They *zzzzz'd zzzzzz'd* all night. You saw to it that the net was carefully anchored all around, yes, indeed, anchored firmly under the thin palette mattress. You would then raise a little bit of it and creep into that extremely narrow bed. Once inside, you tucked the remainder of the net under the palette again and made the effort to go to sleep. You had to be very careful all night not to let any part of your body touch that net, else you would surely be bitten. One night I overheard a conversation: "Shall we eat her here or shall we take her home so the rest of them can have a bite?" Anyway, it seemed that way. Could I have been dreaming?

Not only were there mosquitoes to contend with, but every morning you had to vigorously shake out your shoes lest there be a scorpion hiding in one, ready to do you in with his poisonous sting.

Those were the pests to contend with inside the tent, but everywhere you went there was the buzzing, buzzing, buzzing of flies, trying to light on your skin to bite. Those bites really hurt! In order to distract the flies, you had to wave your hand in front of your face all the time, and all the time, and all the time. This is the Darwin wave mentioned earlier. Interestingly enough, in the movie I recommended earlier, *A Town like Alice,* the heroine is shown standing and talking in an Alice Springs hotel waving a hand in front of her face. I wonder if anyone seeing the movie knew why she was doing it. Of course it was the Darwin wave.

Not only did the area have mosquitoes, flies, and scorpions to contend with, but snakes were common, and you had to be very careful, because every snake in Australia is somewhat poisonous and you were likely to see them in unexpected places. I once looked up at the branch of a tree I was passing under and saw something lovely and green dangling from the branch. I reached up to touch the beautiful thing and, good heavens, it was a snake hanging there in beautiful green camouflage. Then there were, always and everywhere, the ants.

In this country of strange prehistoric animals, there was a profusion of lizards in many varieties and sizes. The frilled lizard would scare you out of your wits, a little thing, not more than twelve or fourteen inches long. If you happened to be anywhere near it to alarm it, it would stand upright on its hind legs, facing you, and open up a wide reddish-yellowish frill on each side of its face, which would widen its face to twelve or more inches, and stare at you, completing its hideous image with a ugly menacing open mouth. Many times I was frightened by one of these hideous creatures.

Another member of the lizard family, the iguana, roamed all of Australia in large numbers, and the Never Never Land seemed to have more than its share. They were usually about twenty-four inches long and were identical to the iguana of our Southwest, but the Australians called them goannas.

The thin, infertile soil of Australia exists only as a sprinkling over a huge, deep bed of sedimentary rock. This rock bed had experienced various shiftings and foldings so that in our area its layers were perpendicular, standing upright with its sharp edges projecting up to the surface. I wore out the soles of my new, heavy uniform oxfords in two weeks. The sprinkling of red dust over the rock bed was anything but stable, and "the red dust of somewhere in Australia" became a familiar phrase in the media.

The hundreds of men in the Adelaide River Army camp were a forlorn, bedraggled crowd. One couldn't help but be touched by the conditions they lived in, and the stresses of their living conditions showed in their faces and bodies. The red dust covered everything, everything, including the men. In that intense heat they wore very minimal clothing; they had to. Their dress consisted of a sleeveless undershirt and a pair of very short uniform trousers. Their hair looked as though they had not had a chance to get to a barber, and most of it was a straggly mess. Sweat poured down their faces and mingled with the red dust that covered them. The worst of it, though, was the prevailing atmosphere of downheartedness, which showed in their faces and their actions.

I stood in line with the men every day for the midday mess. On the very first day I abruptly realized, once again, that you could go around the world to meet the guy next door. Standing ahead of me was the most hopeless figure you ever saw, but in Milwaukee, two blocks from my apartment, he used to stand in front of St. John's Cathedral, facing Cathedral Square, dressed to the nines, striking a pose with his hand in his pocket to show off his stylish gold watch chain, fancying he looked like the famous actor Adolph Menjou. In fact, he was often mistaken for that popular actor. He had beautiful dark auburn hair and mustache, worn exactly in the manner of his hero. He was of the same build as well. He owned 150 suits with top coats and hats and other accessories to match, making a perfect costume every day. He would stand in poses like that for hours at a time and was well known all over Milwaukee's entire East Side. As we stood in the mess line together I said, "Hello! Fancy meeting you here! It's a far cry from Cathedral Square, isn't it?" His face blanched through its coating of sweat streaked red dust, and his jaw dropped. He never said a word, but he turned and left the mess line and I never saw him again in all the six months I was with those lonely, stranded men. How he kept out of my sight all that time I shall never know, but he made a heroic job of it.

It was hard to see that any of the men of this Army unit had a task of any kind to perform. The men had the whole day to themselves. However, with all the secrecy around us, it was hard to know what went on during the night, but I don't think they had any nighttime tasks either. They were just waiting it out, waiting it out, as far as I could see.

One incident which surprised me very much was when a man from one of the tents asked me to come in and see a strange object that had come by way of air from Adelaide. Adelaide is a city in the center of the south coast, and a road, if it could be called such, ran directly north from Adelaide past our camp, and about one hundred miles farther, to end at Darwin on the north coast. Question: Considering all the secrecy around us, how did they get something flown up from Adelaide? Well, I suppose we don't need to know.

The strange object under investigation lay on what passed for a table next to the man's bunk: an egg. "What do you think it is?" he said. "We've been guessing, and we want your opinion. What is this? Some of the fellows think it's an egg. Do you think it's an egg?"

"Yes, I think it's an egg," I replied.

We measured it both lengthwise and in width and measured its circumference. We noted that it was narrower at one end than at the other. We remarked about another feature which should be put into the record: a smooth, hard, stonelike surface. Finally, we concluded by unanimous vote that it was, indeed, an egg. What a satire on wartime deprivation! Needless to say, they kept this foreign object as a precious curiosity, a display piece.

What was my duty with these men? It was to take their minds off their situation, give them something pleasant to do, something pleasant to think about, and if possible bring them a little happiness to keep them from clinical depression, which was a very real possibility at all isolated military bases.

I would sit and talk with them by the hour, something they seemed to need desperately, and they would pour out their hearts to me.

During this time I virtually got down on my knees to thank God that He had given me the vision, the incentive, and the courage to buy that extra footlocker, spend my own money to stock it, run the risk of losing my job because of being INTOLERABLY IRREGULAR, and wheedle and bully that footlocker past every transportation depot halfway around the globe. It is one of the best things I ever did in my life. Its contents were our salvation.

I was told by the Colonel heading the Army unit over in Officers' Country that Australia had expected to be invaded by the Japanese and that in preparation for the assault there was, in this Army camp, a supply of 100 wooden coffins. Thank heaven none of them ever had to be used for their original purpose. I was given a coffin to put in the day room to hold my recreation supplies.

I would cross the footbridge immediately after breakfast in the Officers' Mess pavilion, spread out my recreation materials, and remain with these men until an hour before the evening mess call. I was there with them eight or more hours a day.

What a relief to the men to have these recreational materials! **They could actually DO SOMETHING!** They could laugh sometimes. They played dominoes, checkers, and other table board games, and card games were going on constantly. Groups would gather together with those twelve songbooks, and we'd sing happily every day. I talked with them by the hour, and perhaps this was the most helpful thing I did.

Sunday religious services were conducted in a tent in Officers' Country. The minister was not a chaplain at all but an officer who agreed to accommodate by going through the motions of leading a Sunday church service. Although there was a Catholic chaplain at the camp, I saw him only briefly, from a distance, three times. Talk about reaching out and being helpful; where was he? Music at our Protestant services was provided by playing a miniature portable organ. I was asked to play it for the hymn portion of the worship service but, fortunately, was soon replaced by a serviceman who could make the notes sound far more like music than I could.

An interesting feature of religion on many such camps was a most ingeniously contrived portable, folding three-sided altar. It was like a three-sectioned standing screen, with appropriate religious symbols painted on each section. I once saw an Army chaplain at a different Army installation be a man of three different religions in rapid succession, and he was very devout and sincere in each new role. He donned some appropriate identifying cap or shoulder scarf, opened the appropriate book of rituals, turned the proper wing of the screen toward his new group of worshipers, and became a very sincere, compassionate, and pious priest, minister, and rabbi. This is reminiscent of the work of missionaries where denominational lines are blurred and people gather together to simply worship God.

It was plain to see that means of entertaining these fellows were exceedingly limited. Many an activity that would be considered too boring in other circumstances was welcomed here. One Sunday afternoon when I asked if anyone would like to go on a journey, which really meant to just take a walk, I got a goodly number of takers. You never knew what you were going to see in that strange land, and as we started out we made sure that one of them brought along his rifle in case we might need to protect ourselves. We walked along the edge of the officers' side of the ravine and proceeded some distance beyond the camp, the ravine widening considerably as we progressed. This seemed to be our best route because we could look across the ravine to the enlisted men's side, and this gave us the best viewing possibilities. In the vicinity of the footbridge in the camp the ravine narrowed considerably, but here it was about half a city block wide, perhaps a little wider.

We saw many interesting, unusual things. Everything in the Never Never Land was unusual. Suddenly one of the fellows pointed across the ravine and exclaimed, "Look at that!" There stood quietly as an immobile statue, what must have been the largest goanna in the world. I never knew goannas ever grew that large. It was at least six feet long and stood at least eighteen inches high on its sharply bowed legs.

"Let's hit it," said one of the men.

Another said, "No, let's have Tillie shoot it!"

I readily accepted the invitation, for I knew the animal was perfectly safe with me, who couldn't hit the broad side of a barn door at six feet and who had hardly even touched a gun in her entire life. Always aware of my role as an entertainer, I made a dramatic thing of it, clenching my fist, rubbing my thumb against my nose, and boasting with melodramatic bravado, "Give me that gun. I'll shoot that bastard right behind the ear!"

They patted my shoulder and said, "Go to it, Tillie!"

I lined up the gun sights and fired. To our astonishment the animal fell to the ground, and we scurried down into the ravine and up the other side to inspect it. Lo and behold, wonder of wonders! One chance in a million! I had shot the poor thing right behind the ear, just as I had boasted that I would! Annie Oakley, move over!

The news of this astounding accomplishment spread throughout the entire camp, and the men begged me to stage a marksmanship competition, with all of the men competing with me. Knowing I would never be able to duplicate this fluke of chance, I answered with mock haughtiness, "Oh no, I've made my mark. I don't need to defend my record. Let it stand." I wasn't born yesterday, was I? The men talked about this feat of marksmanship for weeks and weeks.

The climate of the Never Never Land, this back door of nature, was amazing. It was a monsoon type of climate with only two seasons, the wet and the dry. We arrived before New Year's in the dry. It was tremendously hot! Hertha, one of the Red Cross workers, had a thermometer which she set out for an hour on New Year's Day. It registered 114 degrees in the shade. It was an understatement to say that this heat was oppressive. By the time I had been there six months, the season had begun gradually to change to the wet. The monsoon rains that make up the wet are accompanied by fantastically strong winds, so strong that they would bend trees so that their tips might touch the ground. These winds were called "howlin' bobs." One day while I was in the open-sided pavilion which was the day room, one of those howlin' bobs brought in a torrential rain and blew the rain straight through the pavilion, leaving the inside pavilion floor completely dry. So many strange and extreme things in this land! I was told that in the midst of the wet, the ravine was filled to the brim with rushing water and that the entire countryside for close to a million square miles was underwater, which stood, in many cases, knee-high. This was something I had to see to believe. I did see it later and realized that this was, indeed true.

I was told by the Red Cross in Washington to be prepared to live a life of deprivation, but it was a surprise to discover that this meant being totally without outside communication of any kind, including newspapers. We operated in a news vacuum. Ironically, the only newspaper I saw on all of my four stints of duty in Australia was one issue of a gossip-scandal sheet similar to the *National Enquirer* which featured as its headliner a story of the murder of a dear Milwaukee friend and neighbor. A tenant from a rental property she owned, a demented woman, had knocked on my friend's apartment door. The tenant was invited in and then pulled out a concealed piece of lead pipe and pummeled my friend on the head until she died. With that kind of news perhaps it was just as well that other news publications were denied me.

Throughout my entire stay at the camp there were inklings of strange things happening, of unanswered puzzlements which made one wonder what was going on. For instance, one night a veterinarian at the camp who appeared to be simply marking time there announced that he had examined the entrails of fifteen hundred beef carcasses that day. Where did the cattle come from? I learned later that there were some widely scattered cattle stations in the far western part of the Northern Territory, but with very few cattle per square mile because the thin layer of unproductive soil would not support heavy grazing. My butcher says that at a rate of at least four hundred servings of fresh meat per carcass, fifteen hundred carcasses would mean six hundred thousand servings of fresh beef produced that day. In this virtually deserted land, where was the slaughterhouse? Who was to eat all this meat? But you don't ask prying questions of the military. I know we didn't get any of it.

Another puzzle occurred when one day I was standing near the rough dirt road which passed the entrance to our camp and led about one hundred miles due north to the city of Darwin. As I was standing there, a huge truck came lumbering along filled with workmen standing packed like sardines and stripped to the waist because of the extreme heat. Where was that truck going with those forty or so men? One thing I remember still is the sight of a purple shirt blowing in the wind, held by one of these men. What a treat that was, because there was no color anywhere, no color at all. Have you ever thought what it would be like to live with absolutely no color around you? Thank goodness for that yellow-and-green striped strip of canvas I had brought in my footlocker and which I occasionally draped over the back of a chair to afford the enjoyment of some color somewhere. Everything, including the landscape, was olive drab, olive drab. What a sight it was to see that purple shirt! But, what about the truck? One thing which stunned me was that these men waved exuberantly and called out, "Hi, Tillie!" "Hello, Tillie!" How on earth did they know my name?

Another strange, and now in retrospect somewhat ludicrous, event took place a week or two later. I received a personal invitation from some young Red Cross ladies at an Army camp some fifty or so miles away to come for an overnight visit. I accepted happily, though I wondered how they knew my name, as I had never known such a camp even existed. We had a pleasant evening and the Army Major in command of the camp suggested that we all sleep out of doors on blankets spread on the ground. This was surely a novel adventure and it was a memorably pleasant experience, especially inasmuch as the ants which crawled all over the Northern Territory had gone to bed, too. As I prepared to return to my camp the next day, the Major whispered in my ear that he would like me to be his "lady friend." I wasn't born yesterday so I knew that "lady friend" was a euphemism, but before saying yes or no, I played a little game, too: I asked one of the Red Cross girls to find out and let me know if he was married. The word came a few days later that, yes, of course, he was. Nice try, Buster! But again, unanswered questions. What was that camp doing there? And how did they know about me?

Another happening, which was not so puzzling, was an air raid. We scurried out from our pyramidal tents in the dark of night and huddled in a somewhat brushy area expecting that we couldn't be seen. We were not hit, but bombs fell close enough so that we could hear them dropping. Did the Japanese feel they had to deaden the area so that they could, after all, invade? I thought they would have been too busy defending their captured islands throughout the Pacific to be able to even think of preparing to mount an Australian invasion.

We Red Cross women in our compound, surrounded by a six-foot-high tarpaulin to ensure our privacy, were trying to make the best of difficult living conditions, which included coping with personality contrasts. Hertha, the hospital recreation worker, a Red Cross club worker named Flora, and I lived in one of the standard pyramidal tents, and the other was occupied by the social worker, the secretary, and a pleasant, cooperative young Red Cross club worker named Nancy.

The social worker! Good heavens, you never saw anyone like her! Uppity, bossy, fault-finding, holier than thou, always telling people what to do, always criticizing, nobody was ever able to do anything right. She was a tough one to live with, to say the absolute least! The soldiers found her to be the same and they couldn't confide in her. They came to me with their problems, and I would pass them on to Walt to handle in any way he chose.

The secretary, as I have mentioned, was competent in office procedures but absolutely lackluster in personality. She loved to imbibe in alcoholic drinks and from time to time she would become so plastered that I would be called from my bed to go to the Officers' Mess to help bring her back to her tent. Hertha, my tentmate, was always watchful of my morals. I was occasionally called out of bed in the late hours by some officer calling, "Tillie, please come! I need you," so I would crawl out of bed, throw on my coat, and go with him. I suppose the intention was to avoid spreading unpleasant and perhaps harmful news about the poor girl, but her rescuers never told me until I stepped out of the compound to join them that I was needed to help bring the secretary back to her tent because she was dead drunk. Hertha, always suspicious, accused me of being a willing sexual partner available on call at all times.

I finally said to her, "Enough of this! I don't know why the officers always call to me for help when there are four other women available, but I will take you to this last officer who called for me and we'll ask him, point blank, why he called to me."

"Oh, no! I absolutely refuse," she said.

Her sanctimonious, suspicious nature was combined with the fact that, although she was a recreation worker, she refused to walk, even once, over that footbridge and talk with those hundreds of lonely, stranded men. Can you imagine what it was like living in the same tent and trying to keep an atmosphere of pleasant civility? Well, at least I didn't have to live in the same tent with the social worker. I always felt sorry for the secretary and her drinking problem. Maybe the multitude of problems connected with life there were too much for her.

If I live to be two hundred, however, I shall never understand, after MEET THE NEED was so strongly drilled into us, how Hertha, who was waiting to set up a recreation program in a military hospital, the social worker, Flora, and Nancy all insisted on doing nothing rather than giving even one half hour of their time in companionship to these desperately despondent men across the ravine and how Walt, da bigga da boss, sat there in his office tent sending in my reports after deleting my name and replacing it with his but did nothing about the whole situation. The personal relationships among our Red Cross staff were so negative as to be unbelievable. With the exception of the field directors, all the workers in every Red Cross installation I was ever connected with instantly established excellent rapport and developed wonderful and mutually supportive friendships with each other, and it was beautiful to see. The situation at our camp must have been the exception that proved the rule.

In that hot oven of an Army camp, we Red Cross women did have one hour of blessed relief from the heat. To say that we needed it was indeed an understatement, for we could be showered and dried and before finishing buttoning up our uniforms the backs of our blouses would be wringing wet with sweat. Our wonderful relief came in the form of one hour a day for showering. Water was in short supply, making this one-hour allotment necessary. Although we could wash our hands and faces at any time in that old-fashioned granite washbasin on the shelf between the trees, the shower gave us one precious hour of coolness. What would you do in a case like this? Each of us could either have ten minutes of coolness or we could form a wide circle and each of us have a minute under the shower, walking slowly around in that circle until we again reached the shower and our next one minute of bliss. This gave us one minute of cool water followed by five minutes of coolness through the evaporation of the moisture on our skin. This plan worked fine, but what does one do in all of those minutes in between? Perhaps there is a bit of the minx in me, but the others were standing around like sticks so I decided to make it a happy hour. Using my towel, I began a burlesque dance—Gypsy Rose Lee, move over! I manipulated the towel in enticing gestures, remembering the words of the song about the stripper who always managed to stop just in time. I did a dance step all around the shower circle with burlesque gestures such as turning down the corner of my towel, rolling my eyes, and saying such enticing things as, "Hoo hoo!" Naturally, the social worker viewed this with contempt and spat out the word, "Exhibitionist!" The rest of them rather liked it and we had some good laughs. Between the one-minute showering acts, with all of us naked as jaybirds, I did a step used in square dancing called the grand right and left, facing them and clasping each one's hand as I danced around the group. The others laughed heartily and joined in. But oh, how the social worker hated it! So mischievous me, when I came to her, I whirled her round in a dance step and she again spat out, even more venomously, "Exhibitionist!" The others were able to laugh and we had a very good time.

Life at the Officers' Mess, however, was not quite all drab. Every day we did have one good laugh furnished by a dog and a cockatoo, both of which had been living on leftover table scraps from the kitchen shanty, and they both hung around the Officers' Mess area The cockatoo, a large member of the parrot family, was beautiful, with pure white feathers and a yellow cockade. It strutted around with an air of owning the whole establishment. Every morning, right after mess, the dog, as though on schedule, would take a stroll around the mess pavilion. As he came to the front of the pavilion, he was taken by surprise by the cockatoo, which had been waiting for him, also as though on cue, perched on the front wainscot-type wall. The cockatoo flew down, gripping its claws into the fatty skin of the dog's back. The dog bolted away with the cockatoo on his back—the dog yelping, the cockatoo screeching, and all of us laughing our heads off. This comedy act occurred every morning of the entire six months of my stay at Adelaide River.

There was one beautifully bright and memorable day in that half-year. We Red Cross women were invited to spend the day with the U.S. Navy officers in Navy Headquarters in Darwin, located in one of the homes which had been vacated after the bombing of the city.

The city had been completely evacuated, with no grocery stores, no convenience shopping of any kind, and not one civilian living there at all. Have you ever seen a real ghost city? Big buildings like warehouses were boarded up. Many dwelling houses had boarded-up windows. The streets were deserted except for some watchful armed guard or some military person hurrying to a nameless destination. The visit was a strange experience.

It appeared that the Navy officers making up the detachment in Darwin slept in the same house in which they did their office work. Commander Bell, Commander of the Navy installation, was a relaxed, gracious, and friendly host. The other officers were very pleasant and friendly. I was fascinated to meet one of the officers whose name was Fleischacker, a member of the family for whom the famous San Francisco Fleischacker Zoo is named. Two years later when I was stationed in San Francisco, I contacted his wife and we became good friends. The officers were gracious and delightful hosts. They did many pleasant things for us. Among the pleasures they gave us was the wonderful treat of swimming at Manly Beach, which had been a very popular swimming spot prior to the evacuation. The visit was an unforgettable slice of happiness for us. It was a dream day considering the harsh circumstances in which we had been living. The ride of nearly one hundred miles each way was an experience in itself. We rode in the tonneau of a military ambulance which had wheels so high they reached above one's waist, making it adaptable to driving over rough terrain. The unimproved, unpaved dirt road was so rough we were nearly shaken apart. My bosom ached for days afterward. Even though I always wore a brassiere, I am surprised that my breasts weren't shaken off. Still, it was all worth it. It had been a wonderful day, a day to remember.

Some weeks afterward came a very strong request from the Navy office in Darwin on behalf of a battalion of CBs, short for Construction Battalion, and popularly referred to as "Sea Bees." Their role was to build whatever facilities were necessary for conducting military operations, and I suppose they may have had other duties as well from time to time. These Darwin Sea Bees wanted me to be their recreation worker. No, not one of the other Red Cross workers awaiting assignment. They had to have me. No matter what my field director, Walt, said, they insisted on me. He finally gave in and said, "I guess you'll have to go."

There is a grotesque sequel to this story of my life at Adelaide River. Two years later, back in the States and serving as a hospital recreation worker in the Army evacuation hospital named Letterman General Hospital in San Francisco, I was walking along the street one day and I chanced to meet my dear, cherished Red Cross friend Betty Thompson. She was head of the Red Cross Recreation Department at the Navy hospital located at the Navy Pier across the bay in Oakland. She invited me there to visit for an afternoon and evening. It was wonderful to be back with her, even for a few hours.

Since Betty couldn't take off from work, she took me with her on an evening trip escorting entertainers through the wards. Being shorthanded that night, she asked if I would lead one of those groups for her. Of course I would, and my group consisted of a violinist and a vocalist.

Fate directed her to choose for me a certain group of wards which led me to one of the strangest experiences of my lifetime. In one of those wards I happened to notice a man who was all trussed up. One leg, hip, and side were encased in a mammoth white cast with his toes pointing on the bias toward the ceiling. As I passed him, his good arm reached out and he grasped my sleeve and pulled me toward him as he exclaimed, "Tillie, Tillie Jones! I'd know you anywhere, naked or with clothes on!" My first thought was that not only did he have his arm and leg in a cast, but his brain as well, for he surely must be demented to talk to me that way. Then he went on, "I'm Bill, from Adelaide River. Didn't they tell you about me?"

Shocked, I answered no, that I could not remember anyone telling me about a Bill.

I motioned the entertainers to go on to another ward, and he continued with this revelation. "All of us guys at that Adelaide River camp loved you. We just loved you! You know, that hour you had off every day for your shower was the best entertainment in all of the time that we were there. There was a tall tree on our side of the ravine, and if we would climb up it and use binoculars we could see right into your compound. The tarpaulin didn't protect your privacy at all! Oh, that shower! We took turns watching you ladies in that shower. You were wonderful! You were the greatest! What an entertainer! Oh, those dances that you did and that grand right and left that you danced were wonderful. And whirling that social worker—we laughed our heads off. How bossy she was! We all hated her. One of the guys could read lips and we think she kept calling you an 'Exhibitionist.' You were marvelous. You could be a professional entertainer. Oh, you were funny! But look at me! One day you were especially great, and in order to see you better I crawled out too far on the branch and I fell to the ground and broke my hip and my shoulder. They have never knit and now the doctors are making one last try to put me back together again. But I never held it against you!"

I was so offended by this hideous invasion of privacy that I thought to myself, NEVER HELD IT AGAINST ME? MY ACHING CLAVICLE! I HOLD IT AGAINST YOU, DO I EVER! I said good-bye to him and walked on. After I got over my revulsion, I was sorry I had not gone back to comfort this poor man. Think of it, he had been lying like that for two years!

Now I understood why so many people there in the Never Never Land knew me. Gossipy news travels fast, and I must have been a topic of conversation to all the many Army camps scattered throughout the Northern Territory which stood ready for action in case of a Japanese invasion. I must have been renowned everywhere. I could say, like Marilyn Monroe, "Fame, I've had you." Now I knew how those forty men in that truck called out, "Hi, Tillie!" Now I understood that Army Major's attempt to get me to be his "lady friend." I almost felt ashamed that there were not more such offers. I almost wondered, too, if this could have explained why those CBs in Darwin absolutely had to have me, and only me!

As time went on, I began thinking differently about those hundreds and hundreds of men in the camp at Adelaide River. I used to think of them as desolate, lonely, depressed, bedraggled, hopeless, pitiful creatures. If you try, you can find a different way of looking at nearly everything. What young man could be so lucky as to join the Army, travel halfway around the world, live in unique surroundings and an exotic climate, loll in the beautiful sunshine on a white wicker chaise lounge and be entertained every afternoon with a burlesque show complete with naked women and a belly dancer?

X
Ssh! Ssh! It's All a Big Secret!

The author whooping it up with her beloved Sea Bees, Darwin, Australia.

It was not hard to say good-bye to Adelaide River, but it was a challenge to prepare for the ambulance trip to my new assignment in Darwin. How to avoid being shaken to pieces on that rough road? I took two of those cotton diapers I had tucked into my luggage in case of a scarcity of Kotex, knotted them together, and tied them on the bias around my bosom so tightly I could hardly breathe, and I weathered that shaky ambulance ride perfectly. Necessity is the mother of invention.

Darwin was a huge mystery. You did your job and only your job, you looked neither right nor left, and you kept your mouth shut. That was the whole atmosphere. Those were your unspoken orders. You does your thing and only your thing. People all around you were going about their work. I wondered if they knew what they were doing or if they were flying blind like me. There was some logical explanation, apparently, for the presence of the large numbers of Australian Army officers, but I saw no enlisted men. That seemed strange, officers with no enlisted men to lead. When there was something which required an explanation, people would make up some story that you knew was a fabrication, and they always did it with their eyes averted, never looking into your face lest they would give away the fact that it was a fictitious story. Their heads were bowed or turned, too, lest by their facial expression they might give away the great secret, whatever it was. There was also a sprinkling of various officers and other people from strange locations, like a dash of pepper added to some dish you are preparing. There were several English Army officers, a missionary from New Guinea, and various other incongruous people not expected at a United States Navy base.

Other observations that struck me strongly, immediately on my arrival in Darwin, were the many violent contrasts. Here was a lovely city; the white stucco or wooden houses were attractive and often made more charming by flowering tropical vines, mainly the beautiful bougainvillea and other lush flowering greenery. Flowering tropical trees such as the jacaranda and poinciana brightened the landscape. It was such a pretty city, and then to think it was dead! There was not one civilian living in it.

Darwin was the only real city on the entire north coast, and it had been the port of entry for all travelers, being close to Singapore directly to the north. Here was a wild contrast: a large, bustling, modern city, set in the midst of a stone age civilization. The Never Never Land had always been, along with the rest of the continent, the domain of the Australian aborigine, now pushed by the white settlers into this region. It is hard to believe, but these natives were so truly stone-age primitives that they were still making fires by rubbing two sticks together.

Then, too, there was this strange violent climatic contrast between the wet and the dry. Here we were in the very deep tropics, just eleven degrees from the equator. The dry was characterized by its extreme heat, but the wet, for all its howlin' bobs and torrential rains, did have pleasantly mild temperature. The land was just wild, agriculture was impossible and vegetation was sparse.

Here in the surrounding countryside, as at Adelaide River, the underlying folded sedimentary rock was right at the surface, topped by a thin sprinkling of sandy, dusty red soil. There were tufts of grass and here and there a tree or maybe a few scrubby bushes, but that was all.

Except for the harbor, the best physical feature of Darwin was the wonderful ocean beach which stretched westward from the harbor and its Navy Pier. Manly Beach, how lovely it was with its wide, flat stretch of sandy beach, ideal for lounging and playful beach activities, and its wonderful tide. This tide was a spectacular phenomenon, the second highest tide in the world, second only to that of the Bay of Fundy, off the east coast of Canada. I loved to walk barefoot along the beach, having studied the schedule of daily tidal movements so that I would arrive just in time to play my little game with the incoming flow. I would stand at the water's edge facing land and take long steps inland with the incoming tide lapping my heels as I walked. I always wanted to go back and do it again but never had the money for this expensive travel. There never was a truer saying than "No schoolteacher ever died rich."

And where was I to live? My living arrangements were so complicated and fragmented that I was required to compartmentalize my life into four different locations each day. I was to sleep as the only occupant of a lonely wing of the bombed-out hospital. The hospital had been built only shortly before the bombings and had been a source of great pride throughout Darwin. It had been beautiful, with white walls and with wards extending like spider legs from a central administrative core. Parts of it were still usable, and it was still staffed by Australians. Although my ward had been partially destroyed, a part of it could still be used to house that Red Cross gal from the States. I didn't get much rest in my bunk bed, for my sleep was interrupted all night by the clanging wings of a partially destroyed windmill nearby. When I begged that the clanging be silenced, I was met with friendly but almost sneering laughter and a remark to the effect that there were more important things to do. I never had a full night's sleep in all the seven months I was there.

I was to eat at the mess of the chief petty officers of the construction battalion with which I was to work. But this, as my Red Cross recruiting officer would have said, was HIGHLY IRREGULAR, because Red Cross workers were to eat at the Officers' Mess. This was one of the unexplained mysteries of life in Darwin, and when I asked an officer why those regulations had to be ignored, he characteristically averted his gaze, turned his face, and uttered one of those patently artificial explanation common in this atmosphere of secrecy: "Because there are so many visiting firemen that we can't handle it." This was a signal to me that ONE DOES NOT ASK PRYING QUESTIONS REGARDING THE MILITARY. I realized I was fighting a lost cause and that I would have to accept the decision. This turned out, however, not to be a total disappointment, for I developed a wonderful rapport with those dear chief petty officers.

My workday was to be spent running a day room for the battalion, located, as were other Navy installations, at the harbor next to the Navy Pier.

An hour or so before bedtime, I was allowed the privilege of visiting with the Australian nurses who worked at the hospital under the strict supervision of an icy, strictly commanding, stone-faced Matron Mudd. This matron lived alone in a small building nearby. One would have thought I would have lived and slept in the nurses' quarters, but Matron Mudd, as she interpreted her authority and duties, was determined that I, being a representative of a different organization, must bunk in other surroundings. What started out as an arm's length, formal relationship developed eventually into a friendship of sorts. Given her solitary life, she surely must have been a very lonely woman, and she eventually reached out to me for companionship, and we got along well together.

In sum, through this complicated compartmentalization, the planners had managed to account for my entire twenty-four hour day.

Thus it began—my beautiful love affair with the entire Navy Construction Battalion, my adored CBs. No kinder, dearer, more helpful, more considerate men ever lived on this planet. The day room I was to run for them occupied a huge Quonset hut furnished with tables and chairs. There was a waist-high shelf on one side, and near the front door was a chest-high counter with room behind it for supplies. Here I brought my magic box: the footlocker with recreation materials. Without it I could never have operated any kind of a recreation program and would have had to settle for only talking with the guys and being of very limited use to the lonely men I had come so far to help through the rigors of war.

Every morning on the way to the Navy Pier, where all of the Navy offices and my Quonset hut were located, my driver and I passed through empty but still beautiful, silent streets of this skeleton of a city—a modern-day Pompeii, missing only the ashes of a Vesuvius, but with the bombed-out portions of the city acting as a substitute. As we neared our destination, I observed two buildings which became landmarks for me. They were two huge white wooden warehouses standing boarded up and silent. As we passed them I knew we were nearing our destination and gathered my belongings together to begin my daily romantic affair with all those wonderful Sea Bees, as they called themselves. These were mature men, older than the standard run of enlisted men, and true gentlemen. Each one was skilled in some field of construction. They were also polite. The f——word was never uttered, an enormous relief. It helps in difficult conditions to find something to be thankful for.

Each day I arranged on the tables various accouterments for relaxation, playing cards, checkers, other board games, songbooks, a Bible, and anything else I could think of from my magic box. Each day the Sea Bees strolled in. The place was always filled, and they stayed all day and into the evening, leaving only for mess. It seemed peculiar, thinking of it, that a Construction Battalion, which one would think would be working during the day, had their days free. Were they only marking time? There again was another unexplained mystery, but you don't ask prying questions about the military.

It wasn't long before I was visited by a high-ranking Navy officer. He was a little older and quiet, and you could tell he wasn't saying all that he knew, only the necessaries. He sat down and talked with me for nearly an hour. He was pleased with the place and especially pleased with the little red gingham ruffles I had made from that cloth I had tucked into the footlocker and had now placed along the top of the windows of the Quonset hut. They gave a touch of home. Then he got down to work. I knew I was being vetted. These casual visits by the top brass aren't casual at all. They don't waste their time just shooting the breeze with some moll who happens to be working in one of their establishments. He was clever about it, though, and an excellent actor to boot. He kept leading me on about all aspects of my life, and then he would add a few casual comments about himself in order to keep it as a friendly little visit. He asked me where I was born, where my parents' stock had come from—he himself was of French and Belgian descent; what my parents did for a living—his had run a hardware store. He inquired about my schooling, my job, what I thought of my job; he liked his. How did I get into the Red Cross; how he got into the Navy. Did I belong to a church; he himself was a Lutheran. Knowing what the game was, I played it, too. I scrupulously avoided any comment about social issues or political action subjects and, above all, made no comment whatever about anything military. He wanted to know what I thought of my present assignment and the Sea Bees there. Of course I wasn't going to fall into that trap. I simply said they were all very kind and courteous and couldn't do enough for me, remarking that they had even outfitted my little privy out at the back with a seat from a PT boat. No way was I going to speculate as to why a battalion of skilled workmen would just sit around all day with nothing to do. I was able to tuck in a few mild chuckles. He thought he was playing me like a guitar, but I was playing him like one, too. One thing was for sure, though. He was able to walk away with the one thing he had come to find out. I didn't know one blessed thing about the big secret that pervaded our entire lives in Darwin. It must be observed, however, that anyone in or connected to the military in any capacity should keep all viewpoints and comments about social action and political subjects strictly to oneself for the duration of one's service. What the military needs is a cohesive unit with one aim only: to win the war, and any possibility of divisiveness could be a major hindrance to achieving this goal. Thus, his vetting visit was necessary, very necessary.

As the officer left, I again realized that life in Darwin was going on as before, but that the real subject, the core, the reason for it all, was something no one mentioned, and everyone pretended it didn't even exist. Again you remind yourself: you does your thing and only your thing, you looks neither right or left, and you keeps your big mouth shut. At any rate, I'm sure I passed muster, because I never heard a word from the Navy about whether or not I had been accepted. I just stayed on.

A hitherto unused treasure was the collection of Victrola records I had purchased in Washington. The Navy supplied me with the luxury of a record player, and those records were played from early morning until late at night. In the total absence of radios, this was a real treat. Neither newspapers nor television was available either, and we would not have been able to receive any radio program in this remote area, so the Victrola, their only source of music, became an important means of relaxation and musical pleasure for the men.

Adding to the aura of mystery was the daily visit of an Army enlisted man, dressed carefully in full uniform. His daily visit was strange, because I had not seen an Army enlisted man in Darwin and he vanished from sight on leaving the day room. Each day he would play one record, Phil Spitalny and His All Girl Orchestra, which included female vocalists singing popular songs. This orchestra was one of the most popular in the United States at the time. The soldier said to me, "I must come in here. I haven't heard a feminine voice in over a year and this gives me great comfort. I can't do without it. It keeps me sane."

Although the Sea Bees were in the day room constantly in large numbers, occupying all the tables and playing the various games, especially card games, it seemed that they really were there to talk, and talk, and talk. I would sit there by the hour talking with them, and they poured out their hearts to me. It seemed to be an emotional catharsis for them. They would tell me of things they were proud of, things that they regretted in their lives, and how they felt about their experiences.

One day a Sea Bee named Henry Ford brought in a tall, quiet, kindly fellow. I can see him now. He was handsome and had beautiful brown hair and the saddest face you ever saw. He was from Seattle. He had been in the day room often, but this time Henry himself brought him, saying, "Tillie, can you talk with this poor fellow? His wife has just sent him a Dear John letter and he's been in tears ever since." I took his hand and we sat together side by side. All that day and the whole next day, with a perpetual stream of tears, he told me of his whole life, his entire marriage, and everything he could remember about his wife. And she had sent him a Dear John letter. Sobbing, he showed it to me. It read: "Dear George, I feel in all fairness that I should tell you that we are no longer married. I have met a man I want to spend the rest of my life with and I am going to start divorce proceedings. I felt that even though you are far away, it is only fair to let you know, Madeline." I put my arms around his shoulders and did my best to comfort him.

I have a message for all wives or sweethearts whose husbands or loved ones are away on military duty. Wait with your Dear John letter until the poor guy comes home, that is, if he's lucky enough to stay alive until he does come home. It will be far easier for him to handle this terrible news if he is back in familiar surroundings with an established support system in place. And who knows? He may not come home at all and you might not have to even consider writing the letter.

The men away on military duty hang onto their loving relationships with a touching intensity. It seems to be their rock of stability in their perilous world, one thing they can surely count on to sustain them through the vicissitudes of their war service.

Each day I walked over to the sick bay a few blocks away to visit any ill Navy men who might be there. One day the Navy doctor came to the day room and asked if I could please go to the sick bay and break some terrible news to a downed airman because he simply couldn't bring himself to do it. This airman was the only survivor of a crash which had killed all his fellow crew members. I agreed; anything to help. I contemplated how I was going to approach this sad task. Fortunately, on the previous day I had visited a Liberty Ship at anchor in the bay. Incidentally, the crew had given me a whole crate of eggs, twelve dozen, which I very happily accepted—an enormous treat. Any fresh food was nonexistent. I carried the crate back and very ceremoniously presented it to the kitchen crew. They couldn't thank me enough. What we didn't know was that the first layer, amounting to two dozen, was indeed fresh, but all the rest were rotten. What a snide thing for anyone to do, as though life wasn't tough enough. But also, fortunately, the Liberty Ship crew had given me another gift: a bottle of Coca-Cola, absolutely impossible to find, and oh, how the men missed it! I took that bottle of Coke with me and set out for the sick bay. I should have taken the precaution of concealing it, because a Navy man walked along with me begging for that bottle of Coke, saying he would pay me ten dollars for it. I had to explain that it was for an airman whose crewmates had all been killed and that I felt I had to visit him and comfort him the best I could. The man replied that he also thought it was the thing to do. I thanked him for his sacrifice and told him that in any other circumstances I would gladly have given it to him.

So I took the Coca-Cola to the airman in the sick bay. We had a pleasant talk as he enjoyed the Coke. Then I had to break the news the best I could. He sat up in his cot and sobbed on my shoulder. He must have been the recipient of the same counsel that the Marine General Lemuel Shepherd had gone out of his way to give me at Camp Balcombe: You can't let it get you down or you will be overcome with grief, become a casualty yourself and unable to function. You have to say, and mean it, "What a shame. Ping-Pong anyone?" This man said, "How terrible! I would gladly have taken the place of any one of them and I'm surprised to be alive, but that's war," and he finished his Coke.

I was also invited one day to be a guest on board a large Navy vessel docked at the Navy Pier. Before I boarded, a Navy man cued me in on protocol. The captain of the ship says to the visitor, "Glad to have you aboard," and the visitor answers, "Glad to be aboard, sir." I pass this bit of wisdom on to all of you to use when you, too, are invited aboard a ship of the Navy. The visit was short but very interesting, and I was grateful for the privilege.

Since I was the only American Red Cross representative in Darwin, I sent my detailed monthly written reports of all of my activities directly to Channels, and I began writing them as letters beginning: "Dear Channels." I was surprised two years later when, while serving as a recreation worker at Letterman General Hospital in San Francisco, I went to an American Red Cross convention which all were required to attend. At the end of one of the sessions, a featured speaker hunted me up and said, "Hello, Tillie. I've wanted for months to meet you. I'm CHANNELS!" We had a good laugh and a great talk.

Also, since I was the only Red Cross representative in the Darwin area, I knew I would receive some requests which normally would have gone to a social worker or a field director. One surprising request came from a Navy enlisted man who was very worried because the Navy doctor had told him that he had cancer, and he desperately wished for a second medical opinion. Would I make an appointment for a confidential visit to the Army doctor at Adelaide River? I'm sure he didn't realize that this request entailed the rough ambulance ride of nearly a hundred miles each way to make this appointment, as no radios or telephones were in use in order to keep the many Army camps secret and a written request sent through the APO (Army Post Office) would take far too much time. APOs were efficient but understandably slow. The young man knew he couldn't go through Navy channels because he would be told, albeit politely, to put up and shut up, that was the diagnosis, and that was all there was to it. He knew he would have to go outside of the Navy channels, and that's why he came to the Red cross. In order to accomplish this task, I had to request a driver and an ambulance to Adelaide River and back. I could not divulge explicitly the reason for the trip, so I said it was a humanitarian mission, the details of which I was not at liberty to divulge. As the driver and I proceeded on that long journey over the rough road, hardly more than a trail, in our ambulance with the high wheels, I was amazed to see that we were driving through an immense pond of possibility a million or more square miles, which I had always been told we would see during the wet. By this time the wet was at its height. I shall never forget the amazing scene. The water was from six to twelve inches deep, and as we bumped along I thought of my first experience with the typhoon at Adelaide River, with trees bent to the ground and with the howlin' bob blowing the torrent of rain straight through my day room pavilion without leaving a drop of water on the floor. On reaching the camp, I was startled to see the ravine filled to its brim with rushing water on its way to the ocean. I had said I would have to see all of this to believe it, and wow, do I ever believe!

The camp itself was just as I had left it, with Hertha, the social worker, Nancy, and Flora, all sitting on their fannies awaiting assignment, but with THE NEED staring them in the face from across the ravine in the form of hundreds of lonely men, and Walt sitting in his tent-office doing nothing about it.

The rough, bumpy trip back to Darwin completed a long, arduous day, but thanks to my two knotted diapers tied tightly around my bosom, I arrived back in one piece. The young man was brought by the Navy ambulance to Adelaide River at my request because it was a confidential mission and he got his second opinion. I could only assume that all went well, because I never saw or heard from him again.

Back on base, having accomplished my mission, I relived my first experience with a typhoon in Darwin. One day shortly after my arrival, a rather young chief petty officer invited me, after evening mess, to go on a little exploration walk to see what the place was like. I was delighted, it's always good to know where you are. We walked along the ocean shore, and it was lovely in the growing dusk. Suddenly one of those howlin' bobs started up with such terrific wind that it tore at our clothes. We scurried along to see if we could find some kind of cover and discovered a small cave along the ocean shore. We crept into the cave with an air of gratitude to the Almighty for providing us with that respite from the storm. We crouched there while the howlin' bob continued bowing trees to the ground and bringing with it tremendous torrents of rain. When the storm subsided and we started back to the day room, it was, of course, dark and we had to pass an armed guard who demanded the password. My young walking partner later told me that the password changes every day and it was a policy to use words only Americans would be familiar with, such as Philadelphia's *Independence Hall, New York Yankees,* or *Mississippi Delta.* My companion spoke up promptly with the day's password, and our evening exploration walk, which turned out to be unexpectedly adventurous, ended safely.

The evening hours just before bedtime provided me with a welcome gender balance to a day spent surrounded by men. The Australian nurses were cordial, supportive friends, and I still cherish the memory of my hours with them. Occasionally the nurses would arrange a social evening, inviting the Australian Army officers. These were very pleasant social affairs, and I still remember the unusual hors d'oeuvres they served. They were always the same canned (tinned) asparagus spears and Vienna sausages with bits of bread or, on rare occasions, crackers. It was a miracle that they were able to get these treats at all in those days of extreme rationing.

One of the nurses and I endeavored several times to get away from men by bringing a blanket and a couple of magazines to Manley Beach for a little quiet relaxation but were never successful, for we were always joined by Australian Army officers anyway.

It was on one of those excursions that I received my second lesson about a "screw being much better in the tropics, don't you know."

On one of these beach excursions, my nurse friend and I had just spread our blanket and settled down comfortably when a masculine voice behind us asked, "May we join you?"

My friend observed to me, "As you Americans say, the jig is up," and she graciously answered, "Yes, please do."

Our visitors were two pleasant Australian Army officers, and one of them proceeded to fill me in on what life was like in Darwin before the war: "You know the Northern Terit'ry is governed from the national capital of Can b'ra, with the territorial governor and his staff located in Darwin. But you couldn't get office workers, the clarks [clerks], to come here; they just wouldn't come—until the government got the idea of seeing they got a much better screw. And then they came, oh yes they did, by jingo! 'Tis the climate, don't you know." I thought, *the Australians appear to be normal, but flocking to the tropics for a better screw?* I wondered if my education had somehow been incomplete. Could it be that the tropics do give a better screw? It was clearly my turn to comment, but what could I say? Could I risk social calamity by asking what, exactly, has a screw got to do with it? I finally thought of a way to say something without saying anything. I said, "Oh."

One day I was surprised and delighted to receive a written invitation to a formal dinner party to be held in the vacated Northern Territory Governor's mansion and hosted by the Australian Army officers. I was grateful that I had had the foresight to include in my luggage a red crepe afternoon-tea-type dress and a pair of patent-leather pumps. What a fortuitous piece of planning that was, for I was able to arrive as a lady should.

The food was served very formally, in courses. The first course consisted of a little piece of fruit on a small plate. The plate was soon removed and replaced by a second course, which was a small piece of fish. This plate was removed and followed by a small cup of soup. After that was taken away, a small plate with salad was placed before us. Then, and only then, came a medium-sized plate with an entrée on it. After that, a plate with some cooked vegetables, and following that, there was a dessert. Believe it or not, there was still another course—a savory. A savory is a few bites of something like celery or some other raw vegetable to clear the palate, and it was a common custom in Australia to serve a savory at the end of dinner.

A large glass of wine stood at each place, but an officer mentor at my right cautioned me not to take even a sip because we were going to use it later in toasts. Between the courses the many toasts took place and we would raise our goblets and repeat, "To the Captain," or whoever the person being recognized happened to be, and then take a sip. I had been cautioned by my mentor about the type of conversation one uses at formal affairs such as this. The entire atmosphere was to be one of stiff, polite civility, with no jokes and no hearty laughter, that is, not until the toast to the King. There were many toasts, and finally the magic moment arrived. "To the King!" and everybody virtually shouted as they raised their goblets and repeated, "To the King!" and then downed the rest of the potion. After the toast to the King, the entire atmosphere changed instantly from stilted formality, with only impersonal small talk, to jokes, uninhibited laughter, more drinks, and ever more daring conversation until it became a loud, boisterous party.

I noticed that in private parties throughout Australia this structured toasting was customarily followed, though usually less elaborately. There was a toastmaster and his toasts, the party beginning with stiff correctness, and after the final toast to the King, the party became relaxed and the guests became active, often very vocal and even more active indeed.

The formal officers' dinner party gave me a clue about the presence of so many Australian Army officers with no enlisted men for them to lead. They were running the Territorial government because all civilians—among them the Territorial governmental staff—had been evacuated after the bombing of Darwin by the Japanese on February 19, 1942.

Native animal life in Australia is a relic of an ancient age with three man divisions: insects, reptiles, and marsupials. The contingent was attached at one time, say the scientists, to the Asian continent to the north, at a time when these three divisions of the animal kingdom were the norm throughout most of the world. Australia finally drifted southward and was cut off from the Asian continent, complete with its animal inhabitants. Whereas the land north of it, and the other continents as well, lost many of their reptiles and most of their marsupials and developed strains of advanced vertebrates, this did not happen in Australia. The ancient animal groups continue in large numbers to this day, especially in the Northern Territory and in Queensland. The more advanced animal groups were imported and exist mainly farther to the south. There the fragile environment has been pushed by these more advanced species to the very limit of its tolerance, and even its very existence, placing Australia's economy constantly on the razor's edge between existence and extinction. Imported animals such as sheep, cattle, and horses provide the country with its economic existence; and pests, mainly rabbits and the wild dogs called dingoes, dangerously threaten the natural environment as well. In recent years other animals have also arrived on the scene and constitute further environmental problems. Having no natural enemies, all of these animals have proliferated wildly.

Insects in the Darwin area were in great abundance. The blackflies were everywhere, making the Darwin wave necessary constantly to keep them away from one's face. Mosquitoes were not as common in Darwin as at Adelaide River, and we did not have to use the mosquito netting tents over our bunks.

There were other insects, especially ants. The ants were everywhere. I have often said that just as Washington, D.C., is the cockroach capital of the world, Australia is the ant capital of the world, and they hold their worldwide conventions in the Northern Territory. The ants came in a variety of colors. There was the common tan color, the reddish-tan, the black, and, believe it nor not, the white. There is one good thing about ants, though, they do go to bed at night.

Before the wet had set in heavily and while the ground was still not yet under a sheet of water, the Sea Bees invited me on rides into the countryside. I would have planned the excursions myself, but having them to do the planning was even better recreation technique. One day the Sea Bees would not reveal our destination, saying only that we were going to a secret spot, a pilgrimage to hallowed ground. There were a large number of men in our caravan, and we arrived at an area that appeared to contain many tombstones.

I exclaimed, "It's a cemetery! Here?"

The men burst out laughing and shouted, "We fooled you! It's a termite colony!"

Those tombstone-type structures did seem like concrete slabs, rising to rounded top edges about six feet high, three to four feet wide and about eight inches thick, the thickness decreasing as they rose to the peak, making the edges at the top and sides quite thin. The tombstones all faced the same direction, all parallel to each other and with the wide side facing the sun. The men surmised that the construction of the slabs with their widest side to the sun would provide the termites maximum warmth during the wet. How's that for engineering? Colonies of termites lived inside these structures in intricate mazes of tunnels and chambers. I found this to be one of the most amazing sights of my life.

The reptile population was interesting, being made up of snakes and many kinds of lizards. These ranged from a multitude of tiny lizards, to the scary frilled lizards, to the many, many goannas which roam all over Australia. Alligators lurk in the jungelike coastal strip east of Darwin.

Besides the reptiles, the marsupials lived in enormous numbers in the Northern Territory and Queensland. Although there are other marsupials, such as the opossum, most of the marsupials belong to the roo family, and the wide variety of roos is astonishing. There are the six-to-seven-foot-tall black king kangaroos, the six-to-seven-foot-tall red king kangaroo, some slightly shorter kangaroos, multitudes of wallabies, which stand about three or four feet tall, and roos in dwindling sizes to the point were there is even a kangaroo rat.

Kangaroos in Australia's Northern Territory.

One strange animal was a remarkable bat. I saw a colony of them hanging by their tails from the branches of a tree. They can copulate, give birth, and suckle their young while hanging head down from the branches.

On one of the excursions the Sea Bees staged, a large group of us drove over miles and miles of open country and came across a surprisingly large herd of wallabies. We stopped our jeeps some distance away from them and just watched them. They all stood motionless, like statues, and all facing the same direction, giving us a profile view of hundreds of them. This turned into a contest to see which side could stand motionless the longer. Our side finally gave up and drove away because, after all, we couldn't be late for the evening mess.

Birds, yes, and in case one wonders why I didn't mention them before, I'll quote the scientists who say that birds are reptiles that grew wings. Although I saw few birds in the Northern Territory, there were many, many very interesting varieties of birds throughout the rest of Australia. There is the duck-billed platypus, a transitional prehistoric animal combining egg laying, suckling its young, and swimming like a fish. Throughout Australia there are the emu, the kiwi, the fascinating bower bird, the kookaburra, and huge flocks of beautiful parrots which would fly back and forth from north to the south and back again, over the western part of the continent. A tourist to Australia could be captivated by just observing the fascinating wildlife.

The Northern Territory being abo country, I was fortunate to become acquainted with the life of these natives. In fact, I am proud to say I can actually speak the aborigine language. I know one word: *Ah-LAH!* which means "go away!" I learned it from a little nine-year-old abo girl who was placed in the cot next to mine in the bombed-out ward of the hospital. She had been brought there suffering from what the doctors told me were five different potentially fatal illnesses. When the doctors went near her she screamed, "Ah-LAH!" at them. Poor girl, and who could blame her?

The aborigines lived in makeshift huts throughout the Northern Territory, the men hunting, the women digging in the harsh soil for any roots they could find, preparing what passed for meals, and caring for the young. The abos displayed, in their way, interesting exhibits of their artwork, including paintings on rock, intricate pictures in the sand, paintings of native animals on their spears, and painting their own bodies. I was offered the chance of a lifetime: a souvenir to take home. It was a most magnificent museum-quality decorated spear consisting of a shaft of wood about seven or eight inches wide, one or two inches thick, and six or seven feet long. Both edges tapered to a sharp edge, and it was spectacularly decorated with their primitive brown paintings of animals native to the territory, honoring what the abos were killing. I begged permission to take it home in sections, to be reassembled and given to the Milwaukee Public Museum, but was refused because transportation of personal items was not allowed in wartime. What a loss!

I tried, but was never able to master, the techniques of the boomerang, their hunting instrument, which returns to the one who throws it, but I was fortunate to play their didgereedoo. Throughout my many studies I have always been amazed to observe that identical instruments have been invented independently in completely separate civilizations. The didgereedoo is exactly like the Swiss alpenhorn. The size and shape are identical, though the alpenhorn is constructed of the polished metal, a gem of modern engineering expertise. The didgereedoo, however, of identical size, shape and used for the same purpose, was made from a hollowed-out tree branch, narrow at the mouthpiece and widening considerably at the horn end with a gentle near-right-angle upturn. The hollowing out is accomplished by burning and charring a tunnel passage through the entire branch. To play the didgereedoo you sit on a rock or bench, hold the mouth end to your lips, and the horn end will probably touch the ground. You blow into it a sound which is a combination of song and speech, sort of a chant, and it can be heard for miles around. The didgereedoo was used, among other things, for calling tribespeople in the area to a celebration-type gathering called a *korroboree* (core-ROB-oree). Tribal ceremonial dances performed by painted, half-naked men in celebration regalia were prominent features. Other holiday-type activities also took place. I heard of a *korroboree* taking place near our Navy base and asked for permission to attend it but was flatly turned down. I was told that I could never bear to see all that went on and that an orgy of indiscriminate sex was a part of the merrymaking. I don't know if this reasoning was the truth or one of the lame, made-up excuses to protect the all-important policy of absolute secrecy which silently governed our every movement.

Aborigines are not Polynesians but Australasians. The abos were not ignorant, uncivilized creatures. They just lived in a different civilization. Many of them possessed remarkable skills unheard of in our culture. When a crime was committed, people were likely to hire a "black tracker" to find the culprit. I once saw a black tracker on a mission of this kind. Some burglaries had taken place in the nurses' quarters, and the black tracker began by measuring the footprints of the thief, using a twig broken to their exact length. Off he went, barefoot, and in a few days he was back with the thief.

Abos made very good workers on Australian sheep and cattle stations and other places. Australians often told me about them in a very appreciative way. They did mention, however, that one always had to be ready for the excellent worker to end his tenure by walking in to say, "Me go walkabout," and then disappearing on foot and never being seen again.

Chance acquaintances are nearly always pleasant ones, with only very rarely a real bummer. One fascinating visit was that of a New Guinea missionary, not because of the man himself, whose visit to the day room was too short to get to know him, but because of what he brought with him—a masterpiece of linguistic invention. It was a homemade combination songbook and prayerbook, also containing sections from the Bible, and all in pidgin (pronounced pigeon) English. This scaled-down and somewhat altered English, usually accompanied by appropriate explanatory gestures, was, and still is, widely used by traders and missionaries as a means of communication with people speaking different languages along the China coast and throughout the Pacific islands. The songs were complete with the melodies carefully written on the standard musical scale, and included the Gloria Patri, the Doxology, and some best loved hymns. Selected Bible passages included the Ten Commandments, the Beatitudes, some Psalms, the familiar funeral words of comfort, "Let not your heart be troubled . . . ," and various other most loved devotional selections. The main prayer was, naturally, the Lord's Prayer, and there were other carefully chosen ones, all in pidgin English. The translators had managed, using this greatly abbreviated and altered English, to convey the full, true meanings, and do it with a touching and tender reverence. The book was a masterpiece. I was enchanted and pleaded with the missionary to let me copy the Lord's Prayer, but, can you imagine, he snatched the book from me and disappeared in a huff. I still cannot figure out why. I did, however, remember how the prayer began: "Numba one boy (with arm and forefinger pointed heavenward) belong me (finger pointed to chest)." I still, sometimes, start my own Lord's Prayer that way, and regret that I must continue in our own less colorful English.

Throughout my several careers, I have, on rare occasions, observed a striking phenomenon. In spite of all our education and all our efforts and successes in controlling our emotions, they sometimes play tricks on us. Especially when one is under stress, an unexpected sight or occurrence can trigger a spontaneous emotional response, unintended and shocking to the person experiencing it. Our emotions at that moment are out of control. The incident I am recounting occurred on a Darwin street. People in uniform talked with each other when meeting casually on the street and elsewhere, and it seems that everyone stopped to greet a woman in uniform. I had just received a wonderful gift from two dear Milwaukee friends, a package of cosmetics containing a little box of face powder, some rouge and lipstick, and a tiny bottle of Lily of the Valley perfume. The gift was an enormous treat in circumstances in which doing without is the name of the game, and the next day I added a little dot of the perfume to my morning toilette and walked along the street with a new bounce in my step and an increased optimism in my outlook. That was what the perfume did for me.

However, it did something entirely different for a friendly but very formally sedate English Army officer with whom I regularly exchanged greetings. He suddenly started crying, put his arms around me, and sobbing uncontrollably burst out, "Lily of the Valley! It reminds me of home!"

I consoled him the best I could. "Go ahead and cry. We all need to, sometimes. I've been away from home a long time myself, and I know just how you feel."

After a few minutes he said, "I'm all right now." He drew himself up to his full height, straightened his lapels, donned his customary armor, his veneer of strict formality, and walked on. Poor man, my heart went out to him as it did and still does, to everyone on duty far from home. You're always lonely, even in a crowd.

I have been propositioned by experts, but this one surely would win the International Prize for Creative Propositioning. This creature was a pharmacist and we met often on the street. We began saying hello to each other, and the hello gradually expanded into some small talk: "Nice day," etc. One day, though, the hello was immediately followed by, "If you will be my bed partner, I'll furnish you with all the toilet paper you'd like."

I was so infuriated that my first impulse was to slap his face, but ladies don't slap faces, so I settled for, "I'm going to have to disappoint you, but I'm not for sale. Whatever gave you the weird idea that I was?"

"Just thought it was worth a try," he answered, and I had to hold myself back, again, from slapping him.

After that when we met, it was only hello and we'd walk on. It must be observed, however, that his offer was not without merit, for Australian toilet paper was a pathetic imitation of the real thing. It existed as rolls of crinkled rice paper, and once you've seen rice paper, you'll never forget it. It is almost transparent, with a natural glaze that resembles that of wax paper, and it is absolutely nonabsorbent. Using it was a real sacrifice. When I was a child on the farm in Wisconsin, we did better than that with the previous season's Sears and Roebuck and Montgomery Ward catalogs hanging in our two-holer privy, and when our family of nine had exhausted them, we resorted to corn cobs from a bucket in the corner. The corn cobs really weren't bad if you were gentle about it; they beat the rice paper all hollow. In later reflections about the pharmacist, I couldn't help conjecturing that he might have had better luck with his next prospect if he had thrown in some Kotex as a bonus.

With Christmas coming on, we were hard put to think of a way to celebrate the holiday. How does one celebrate Christmas in an isolated land like that one? We put our heads together and planned a gigantic, bang-up Christmas party for the whole Sea Bee Battalion. It all centered on a Christmas tree. We simply had to have a Christmas tree, for what is Christmas without a tree? So we made our own. Again, necessity is the mother of invention, so the men brought in a bathroom plunger and suctioned it onto counter in the day room so it couldn't help but stand firmly upright. We next made a ceremonial excursion to the jungle growth extending along the coast eastward from Darwin and cut some leaves of the pandanus palm. These leaves have a two to two-and-a-half-feet-wide flat, circular shape, with waxy green spikes extending outward from the central spine, narrowing gradually to a sharp point at the tip. The men cut these spikes into varying lengths and wired them around the handle of the plunger, starting with the shortest spikes at the top and gradually widening the tree as they progressed downward. They produced a remarkably convincing and beautiful Christmas tree. We decorated the tree with our jewelry; little strings of my pearls and the men's short silver and gold chains provided the garlands, and from its branches hung silver and gold rings, some set with gems. It was a triumph. The mess cook sifted the weevils out of the flour and produced fine, huge sheet cakes complete with frosting. We cut the cakes into many pieces so that each celebrant could have a piece of Christmas cake. The men ceremoniously gave me two pieces of the decorations they had made and placed on the tree: a ring and a pendant with the Sea Bee logo incorporated in it. I still have them and I wear them in reverent memory every Veterans Day and Memorial Day. We danced and sang the whole evening. I danced with every one of them, the men danced with each other, we sang songs, and again I thanked the good Lord for the phonograph records. It was one of the best Christmas celebrations of my entire life.

I was with these wonderful men for seven months, but as time went on I realized that I had developed a condition which required surgery and a stay at the U.S. Army Hospital in Brisbane. I had to leave my footlocker with its recreation supplies behind, as well as nearly all my belongings, bringing only an overnight case, knowing I would be back in a short time. As fate would have it, I was never able to return.

My flight to Brisbane was in the very same single-engine plane in which we Red Cross women had been flown to Adelaide River. I almost refused to board the plane, remembering how I had vomited all the way across the Great Desert of Australia. How did I know it was the same plane? I saw the repair that had been made at Longreach after the eagle had flown into its wing.

My seatmate on the trip was a Baptist minister who took pains to tell me that his parents were not descended from convicts. When we touched down at a lonely air strip in the Far Outback for lunch and refueling, he made it a point to sit beside me and instruct me on Australian protocol. We lunched at a table in a small galvanized corrugated metal shack and were skillfully served by an excellent waiter. This partner of mine said, "Thn-kew," every time the waiter placed anything before us or removed anything from us. I couldn't for the life of me join in his "thn-kew" chorus, so he thn-kewed the waiter for himself and for me. Therefore, with everyone else also showing the customary attempts at politeness, all we heard at the table was a rain of thn-kews, thn-kews, thn-kews, and conversation was impossible. Immersed in the class system of England, the Australians attempted to carry out its customs. It must be said in all fairness, the class system of the Aussies was not as rigid, however, as was that of the English. Still, aspects of it surfaced from time to time. You said thn-kew to anyone making any gesture of a service nature for you, waiters, maids, elevator operators, and the like all got the treatment, rubbing it in over and over that they were only of the servant class. A true thank-you was reserved for people of your own class. As we rose from the luncheon table, I said to the waiter, "I do appreciate your excellent service and thank you for it." He responded with touching gratitude at being treated for once like a fellow human being. The tip I gave him didn't hurt either.

The Big Secret Revealed at Last

It was in a ward at the U.S. Army Hospital in Brisbane that I learned THE BIG SECRET OF DARWIN. Darwin was one of the three secret bases for the liberation of the Philippines. The second base was Perth, three-quarters of the way down the west coast, where the finest torpedo man in the entire Navy spent several days at a time every week or so when he was not at our Chief Petty Officers' Mess in Darwin. Navy veterans I have talked with say the third was Brisbane, the site of an important American submarine base. The United States had three submarine bases in Australia: at Darwin, Perth, and Brisbane.

The unlocking of the secret of Darwin was done by two ladies who were fellow patients in my ward. They were there with the nine-month-old baby of one of them, and their husbands were patients in a different ward of the hospital. The two families had been leaders of guerilla warfare in the Philippines. The Japanese had identified them and were pursuing them with the intention of killing them. They managed to always be on the move, always a day ahead of the Japanese, along with a water buffalo they took with them to provide milk for the baby. Finally, they were evacuated by submarine and brought to Darwin and then to Brisbane for health checkups, minus the buffalo, of course. These ladies told me that as soon as night fell Darwin erupted into a beehive of feverish activity. Troops poured out of the boarded-up warehouses and other buildings, and submarines were unloaded and then reloaded with troops, guns, ammunition, and other supplies. The darkened city swarmed in activity, all in a complete blackout. The entire operation was planned and directed from Darwin. The U.S. Navy bases at Perth and Brisbane played only a small part in the operations, their participation occurring only as loading and unloading submarines at night.

Now, at last, I understood the Darwin secrecy: the Sea Bees apparently working at night and resting in the daytime, the averted gaze when phony explanations were given, the reason why I was not allowed to eat at the Officers' Mess; the armed guards at night demanding the daily password; the Adelaide River veterinarian inspecting fifteen hundred beef carcasses in one day. The whole jigsaw puzzle coming together at last. However, the Army enlisted men at Adelaide River were not a part of the Philippine liberation movement at that time. They were there, along with many men in such camps dotted throughout the northern portion of Australia, to repel an expected full-scale invasion of Australia by the Japanese.

Imagine my surprise on discovering that Steve, the handsome, athletic, tight-lipped chief petty officer who occasionally joined our mess, was really a lieutenant commander who masterminded and commanded the entire operations of the three bases, and all the planning and orders came from Commander Bell's so-called lodgings, which in reality were also the headquarters for it all.

The Japanese never knew where the bases for the guerrilla activity were located, for if they had, they would surely have bombed us all into eternity. In retrospect, one cannot help being amazed at the extreme daring of this whole operation and appreciate the tremendous need for secrecy. Actually, our lives were in our hands all of the time, although many of us never knew it.

I had received a written commendation from the commanding officer in Darwin for my work there, so you could say I had received a written commendation for not knowing what I was doing! Doesn't that unique accomplishment belong in the *Guiness Book of Records?*

XI

Toowoomba, Good Place to Sit Down

View of Table Top Mountain, Great Dividing Range, viewed from The Overlook, Toowoomba, Queensland, Australia. The Table Top was the locale of the author's weekly picnics.

Although I had every intention of rejoining my dear Sea Bees in Darwin after my surgery, this was not to be. I was sent to run a recreation program in tandem with a Navy Chief Petty Officer at an R & R resort for submariners in the lush climate of Toowoomba, fifty miles inland from Brisbane.

Toowoomba is an aborigine word meaning literally "good place to sit down." In other words, good place to make camp. In fact, it was, and still is, a good place for getting away from it all: the heat, the limited vegetation, the desert and near-desert conditions, and the insects. Truly an escape to comfort and beauty. It is located on a plateau overlooking the Great Dividing Range. Although it rests on the Tropic of Capricorn at the edge of the torrid zone, its elevation gives it milder summers than places at lower levels, while keeping winters, although cool, warm enough to encourage year-round plant growth. Its elevation and nearness to the ocean guarantee sufficient rainfall to sustain this beauty.

Toowoomba was charming without being pretentious. The heart of the city contained the usual public buildings, all of them attractive, some good department stores, and other edifices, including a very large, handsome hotel where a feminine guest could protect the pristine purity of her reputation by checking into a room on the "Women Only" floor.

Most of the residences were far from palatial, mainly comfortable and somewhat modest homes complete with picket fenced dooryards planted not with grass, but with a profusion of garden flowers. Very, very English and very, very charming, don't you know.

Some people call Toowoomba the American city because its vegetation seems to be more American than Australian. The soil is somewhat deeper there than in the rest of the country and is more productive. The adequate rainfall made it possible for a wide variety of trees to flourish there, and for once I didn't see a single eucalyptus, also known as the gum tree. If it weren't for the eucalyptus, the rest of Australia would just about have to do without trees at all, because that tree is amazingly able to survive in near-arid conditions, with its gray peeling bark and its long fingers of pale gray-green leaves hanging listlessly from its branches. They would never dare spread themselves flat because they would be burned up by the hot sun. That tree is a very interesting vegetative adaptation. But here in Toowoomba we didn't have to depend on that bedraggled specimen of a tree, and the delightful variety lifted the heart and spirits. Flowers thrived all year in great, joyous variety and abundance. Standard summertime flowers flourished and, in what passed for winter, there was a profusion of plants which did well in cooler weather. Freesia was one, and all of the varieties of bulb plants made the winters beautiful. Our spring flowers such as tulips, daffodils, and hyacinths were a winter joy in Toowoomba. Calla lilies grew in such abundance that they were commonplace, not the occasional expensive specimen reserved mainly for bridal bouquets as is the case with us. The people of Toowoomba were devoted and passionate gardeners, and roses were favorites with them. Everyone grew flowers, and a favorite entertainment at an afternoon tea party was a garden walk. Again, you could almost think you were back in Mother England.

Our Navy R & R resort took up the entire area of the recently laid out Newtown Park, on the outskirts of the city. Our buildings consisted of an extremely large recreation and mess hall with an attached kitchen. The building faced the entrance to the park, and farther back there were many small sleeping cabins. These cabins were divided, each one being a small double house furnished with two-tier bunk beds. Some of these cabin sections slept two; some slept four people.

Our combination recreation room and mess hall consisted of one immense room large enough to accommodate tables for dining and table games and still leave a very large open space for table tennis and other such games, plus a large space for dances. The entire wall at the far end of the room was occupied by a huge stone fireplace with stonework extending to the outer wall on each side and a mantel shelf which stretched across the room. On the wall above was displayed a memento from each submarine crew that had vacationed there. This memento consisted of a thirteen-inch square, dark brown wooden plaque which we furnished, and every submarine crew gave us its decorative logo to attach to it. Each submarine in the fleet had the name of a certain fish, and although I know there are many varieties of fish, I am still surprised at the great number of different names they came up with. The R & R resort had been in operation five months before I arrived, and I was stationed there for seven months. By the time I left, there was space for only three more on the entire wall, and the R & R operation continued with plans to use an adjoining wall for additional plaques after I left.

Twenty-three months of combat duty entitled a Navy man to two weeks of R & R. However, because submarine duty was extra stressful due to cramped quarters and great constant nervous tension, it was necessary to provide two weeks of R & R after every patrol, which lasted ninety days or less. A man's R & R was a time of complete rest, relaxation, and constant entertainment which he could participate in or not as he chose.

A Navy officer was in command of our operation, and he occupied a combination office-and-bunk house near the recreation hall. There was a competent chef with kitchen helpers, and a highly adequate maintenance staff so all of the mechanical aspects of our service went like clockwork.

Lillian "Tillie" Jones with submariners at R & R resort, Newton Park, Toowoomba.

The recreation part of our R & R was conducted by a two-person team: a Navy Chief Petty Officer named Burdette Harrison and a Red Cross Able Bodied Rec named Tillie Jones. We made a wonderful team, we worked hand in glove. Burdette was an excellent recreation leader, always cheerful, always putting the positive outlook on everything, and to top it off, he was a wonderful piano player—an expert with popular music. His home was in San Francisco, and he had a beautiful young wife who became a good friend of mine when I was later stationed there.

Most of the recreational activities were well in place by the time I arrived. We offered unstructured casual Australian experiences which were just there for the viewing and for the fun of it, and we ran a series of large-scale planned activities as well.

The Sea Bees' pet king kangaroo at R & R resort. Their pet tomcat watched the "roo" work out with his punching bag.

The casual offerings were unusual, very Australian, and delightful. We had an aviary, as big as a large living room, complete with a tree and an amazing variety of small, colorful Australian birds. Men watched them for hours, the birds were indeed highly interesting.

We had two pet kangaroos, one a six-foot-tall brownish-black male king kangaroo and one somewhat smaller female. They were both very tame. We fitted the male with small boxing gloves, the men boxed with him constantly, and their cameras were always snapping their pictures. The female came complete with a young one called a joey. This baby was well enough developed so that it was no longer attached to the nipple inside the mother's pouch. When a kangaroo is born, it is about the size and shape of a peanut. The mother secretes a moist, slippery substance which she spreads with her front paws from the vaginal opening to the pouch. The baby slides down in it and enters the pouch, searching about for the tiny knob within which is its nourishing teat. The baby puts its mouth around this nipple, which swells so much that the young one can never get it out of its mouth, thus ensuring that it will never lose its source of sustenance. The teat grows with it, but at last the joey is large enough and can open its mouth far enough to leave the nipple temporarily and explore the outside world. This little joey of ours came out and hopped about the immediate vicinity from time to time, then dived back, headfirst, into the pouch for lunch and a nap. The men kept their cameras busy with photographs of themselves with the mother and her joey. They had wonderful relaxed fun with those roos.

Walks into the city were common, and there was also an opportunity to rent riding horses from a neighbor.

One of the most popular services we offered was mending the men's clothing. Once a week a rather large group of ladies spent the day with us and

Submariners playing with their pet mother kangaroo and her little "joey," R & R resort.

mended anything the men brought them. At noonday mess, the ladies sat among the vacationers, and they continued stitching throughout the afternoon. Many men sat by them during the day just talking with them as though they were their mothers. The ladies also attended many of our evening activities and the men loved it. Those dear ladies greatly enjoyed a taste of American cooking, and they looked forward to having noontime mess with us. We furnished each one with a tea bag so that every one of them could steep her own cup of tea, but we soon learned that we needed to furnish each with two tea bags because at first they wouldn't use theirs, drinking the plain hot water so they could take the tea bag home as a curiosity.

We had entertainment going on every evening. Two nights a week it was penny bingo, two nights a week a dance with an orchestra, and the other three nights were given over to impromptu, informal partying. We had plenty of willing young ladies who volunteered to come and dance or spend an evening with the guys, and the dear Australian women who did all of that mending came also for the bingo and the informal parties. We didn't need to worry about being repetitious because the men all had a very good time, stayed only two weeks, and went away happy, knowing they had been treated like royalty, coddled, pampered, thoroughly spoiled.

The informal parties were probably the best nights of all. With Burdette happily and effortlessly ringing out the tunes, we sang the popular songs of the day. "Mairzy Doates and Dozey Doates and Little Lamsy Divey" was one of the favorites, as well as "Don't Sit under the Apple Tree," "The White Cliffs of Dover" "Praise the Lord, and Pass the Ammunition," and many others. Many songs to which we did not know the words rang out from Burette's piano, with anyone who knew a few of the words singing them when they could. The Australians taught us three of their favorites, too. One was an English sailors' song that went: "Singing bell-bottomed trousers, coats of Navy blue, he'll climb the riggin', like his daddy used to do." Another very popular one was "Bless them all, bless them all, the long and the short and the tall, bless the sergeants and W-O-Ones, bless all the corporals and their blinkin' sons, for we're saying goodbye to them all, as into their billets they crawl. There'll be no promotion this side of the ocean, so cheer up my lads, bless them all." No party was ever complete without the trademark of every Australian: he sings "Waltzing Matilda." Furthermore, now that we were living among the Aussies in Toowoomba, we followed the maxim, "When in Rome, do as the Romans do," and now that we were here, we were going to be Aussies with the rest of them. So here's "Waltzing Matilda" so that you, too, can become an Aussie with the rest of us:

> Once a jolly swag man sat by a billabong,
> Under the shade of a koolibah tree,
> And he sang as he sat and waited 'til his billy boiled,
> You'll come a waltzing, Matilda, with me.
>
> Waltzing Matilda, waltzing Matilda,
> You'll come a-waltzing, Matilda, with me,
> And he sang as he sat and waited 'til his billy boiled,
> You'll come a-waltzing, Matilda, with me.

Up came a jumbuck, drinking at that billabong,
Up jumped the swag man, one, two, three,
And he sang as he tucked that jumbuck in his tucker bag,
You'll come a-waltzing, Matilda, with me.

Waltzing Matilda, waltzing Matilda,
You'll come a-waltzing, Matilda, with me,
And he sang as he tucked that jumbuck in his tucker bag,
You'll come a-waltzing, Matilda, with me.

Up came the landsman, mounted on his thoroughbred,
Up came the troopers, one, two, three,
Where's that jolly jumbuck you've got in your tucker bag?
You'll come a-waltzing, Matilda, with me.

Waltzing Matilda, waltzing Matilda,
You'll come a-waltzing, Matilda, with me,
Where's that jolly jumbuck you've got in your tucker bag?
You'll come a-waltzing, Matilda, with me.

Up sprang the swag man, jumped into that billabong,
You'll never take me alive, said he,
And his ghost may be h-e-a-r-d as you p-a-s-s by that bill-a-bong,
You'll come a-waltzing, Matilda, with me.

Waltzing Matilda, waltzing Matilda,
You'll come a-waltzing, Matilda, with me,
And his ghost may be h-e-a-r-d as you p-a-s-s by that bill-a-bong,
You'll come a-waltzing, Matilda, with me.

Note: A swag man is a wandering traveler living off the land. A swag, itself, is all of your possessions, which are carried in a bag on your back. A billabong is one of the many small ponds scattered here and there in the Bush and occasionally in the Outback. A billy is a straight-sided tin pail with a wire bale handle, used for boiling tea water over a campfire. A jumbuck is a sheep. A landsman is a landowner. The troopers are the police. So what's waltzing Matilda got to do with it? It's just an Australian saying with no particular meaning.

Now that you can sing "Waltzing Matilda" and know it by heart, you're not far away from becoming a dinky di Aussie, fair dinkum.

Occasionally some Australian would come up with a comic song or story which would bring the house down in riotous laughter. One that topped the list was "Oh gorr blimey, 'ow ashimed Oi waws." It went like this:

> Oi kissed her on the wrist, 'ow ashimed Oi waws,
> Oi kissed her on the wrist, 'ow ashimed Oi waws,
> Oi' kissed her on the wrist; she said, "Oi cahn't resist,"
> Oh gorr blimey, 'ow ashimed Oi waws.
>
> Oi kissed her on the arm, 'ow ashimed Oi waws,
> Oi kissed her on the arm, 'ow ashimed Oi waws,
> Oi kissed her on the arm, she said, "Twill do no 'arm,"
> Oh gorr blimey, 'ow ashimed Oi waws.
>
> Oi kissed her on the knee, 'ow ashimed Oi waws,
> Oi kissed her on the knee, 'ow ashimed Oi waws,
> Oi kissed her on the knee, she said "Ow far can you see?"
> Oh gorr blimey, 'ow ashimed Oi waws.

By now you get the drift, and you realize why I made a strong successful effort to forget the rest of the song and its logical conclusion. However, when you go to Australia, you might want to find someone who knows the whole bawdy song. I suppose it wouldn't hurt a person to hear it just once. By now you have also concluded that the standard level of socially acceptable humor in Australia was a bit lower than in the United States.

Our evening parties always ended up with spontaneous dancing to Burdette's peppy piano music. Those parties were the best and the most fun of the entire week.

Once a week I rounded up many takers for a picnic. We started out with some tucker for each man, tied neatly in a red bandanna tucker bag, and were escorted in jeeps to a spot on the far western edge of the city, the Overlook, where we viewed one of the most spectacular scenes in the world. When you are a tourist to Australia, don't miss it. The plateau on which Toowoomba rests drops sharply, straight down many hundreds of feet, to an expanse of level land stretching for miles, farther than the eye can see. Rising from the floor of this depression are individual hills high enough to be classified as mountains. This is the Great Dividing Range, old and worn down, similar to our Appalachians but not nearly as high. Our Appalachian mountains, however, stretch in long parallel ridges, differing in this respect from the many single mountains of the Great Dividing Range.

Three of these mountains rose quite near us, and it was the middle one which we chose for our picnics. It is called Tabletop because the top of it is large and absolutely flat, making it an ideal spot for picnics, and it is accessible by foot.

Once there, we thrilled at the magnificent views all around us. I drew the men out in conversation, each telling about himself, and we established a friendly, easygoing rapport. We boiled our billy, made our tea, ate our tucker, and then I set about turning them into Aussies, and they loved it. I explained the rudiments of the cockney dialect and illustrated it with Australian stories, Aussie style. I gave each man a leaflet which would help him become a dinky di Aussie. This is the leaflet:

How to Be an Aussie

- It isn't an elevator, it's a lift.
- It isn't a truck, it's a lorry pronounced lorrrry.
- It isn't aluminum, it's al-you-minnie-um.
- It isn't the black top, it's the bitch-you-min.
- It isn't food, it's tucker.
- Genuine is dinky di, and honest to goodness is fair dinkum.
- It isn't Bris-bane, it's Brisb'n.
- The national capital is not Can-berra, it's Canb'ra.
- It isn't strawberry, raspberry, etc., it's strawb'ry, rahsb'ry, blueb'ry, gooseb'ry.

- It isn't, "Let's try it, pal," it's "Give it a go, mite" (mate).
- To be an accomplished conversationalist, you tuck in the phrase "don't you know" every chance you get, as in "Ever so lovely, don't you know."
- You don't say, "So long," or, "Goodbye," you say ta-ta and pronounce it taht-ah.
- It isn't a dam and a hydroelectric power plant, it's a scheme.
- Fine boys and girls are bonza lads and lassies.
- To be polite, you must never say "bloody," so every other word you utter must be "bloody."
- If you're knocked up, you aren't pregnant, you're completely exhausted.
- If you're sick, you're crook.
- You don't say, "Oh my goodness," you say "Oh gorr blimey."
- Every member of the animal kingdom is a "jolly" someone or something or other, as the jolly Americans, the jolly Cricket team, the jolly horse . . . you get the idea.
- A horse race is a rice mee-ting, usually held not every two weeks, but every fortnight.
- Home isn't your house in Australia, home is England.
- Your evening meal isn't dinner, it's tea.
- It isn't the movies, it's the cinema.
- A workman of any type is a digger.
- A man isn't a guy or a fellow, he's a bloke.
- They're not sheep ranches and cattle ranches, they're sheep and cattle stations.
- He didn't steal it, he lifted it.
- If you have a scone in the oven, it might mean you're pregnant.
- It isn't a hot dog, it's a savaloy.
- You don't say, "Yes, I agree," you say, "Right-o," and you pronounce it Roight-o.
- If you emphatically agree, you say "too roight."

(Ladies, I didn't tell this to the fellows, but I'll tell it to you: it isn't your pussy, it's your keester.) If you do all of these things on this list, speak cockney, and sing "Waltzing Matilda" with gusto, you're well on your way to being a dinky di Aussie, fair dinkum. Too roight, mite!

Those picnics were memorable, an experience of a lifetime. I was able to buy an oil painting of the scene from the Overlook, and it is one of my most treasured possessions.

While the wonderful Australian ladies weren't with us at our R & R mending the submariners' clothing, mothering them and playing bingo and singing along with us, they were working for our men at home. One of them had a pattern for a handmade koala, similar in size and shape to our popular teddy bear, very convincing in appearance, well made, and utterly delightful. The ladies sold them at a very low price: the cost of materials plus a pittance for their work. Many a vacationer wanted one sent home. The orders poured in, but how was the man's family to receive them? Oh yes, the Red Cross, of course, and that meant me. I spent my entire salary buying the wood to make shipping boxes and then making up for unexpectedly high or inadvertently forgotten shipping charges and sometimes the unintentionally forgotten cost of the koala itself. And who made the boxes? You guessed it. Little ol' me, from over the sea. Oh well, *c'est le guerre.*

Remember what I told you about field directors? My luggage, which I had to leave behind in Darwin, arrived in due time, and you can guess how delighted I was to see it, for I had been making do with very minimal personal supplies carried in that overnight case. Imagine my surprise and horror, though, on seeing that my extra footlocker, my magic box full of recreation supplies, was completely empty, with the exception of that lone strip of colored seating canvas. The explanation came in the next day's mail in the form of a letter from a Red Cross friend. A new field director had arrived on the scene and he had forced the lock and scattered the contents far and wide, never contacting me, though others had no trouble in corresponding back and forth with me. I happened to see that miserable excuse for a man one day on an errand in Brisbane and I confronted him, telling him I had bought all of those supplies myself, with my own money, except for two Red Cross game books which Joe Gralnik, Supervisor of all Red Cross activities in that entire region of Australia, had given me, along with congratulations and enthusiastic permission to transport and use the footlocker and its contents in any way I felt appropriate. The creep never apologized and never offered to reimburse me. The only thing he said was, "Don't tell Joe." I didn't tell Joe, but only because I never saw him again. My, he was a wonderful man, Joe Gralnik. A highly educated and widely experienced social worker from Chicago and one of the most gracious, perceptive, and understanding persons I have ever known. I knew him and his beautiful and lovely wife, Ro, in Washington during that five-month indoctrination marathon. They both had volunteered for Red Cross overseas duty, and Ro had been sent to the European theater, while Joe was posted in Australia.

They say it takes all kinds to make a world, and I suppose it does.

All in all, the Toowoomba stint must rank as an ideal assignment, though I suppose there has to be a fly in just about every ointment. Thank goodness mine was a very small fly, but it was there just the same in the person of the chief cook, an early-middle-aged career Navy man who believed that neither the military nor the quasi-military, which I represented, was any place for a woman, and who felt it his bounden duty to prove it. Nothing personal, you understand, oh no, but just as a policy. From time to time I was confronted with small inconveniences, studiously never large enough to merit a complaint to the Navy officer in charge of the camp, but clear enough so that I would get the message. In a way, it was rather funny to see what pains he would take to think of something that could be annoying but not bad enough to get him into trouble.

Our huge recreation-mess hall was well constructed, but it had one major flaw: it had no ventilation system, no exhaust fan to rid the place of smoke fumes. As I have mentioned, smoking was a virtually universal custom in the culture of the time, and the stresses of military duty intensified the habit. A person observing our Toowoomba R & R would have immediately remarked, "You can say that again, sister, doubled in spades." The air was thick and blue with cigarette smoke all the blessed time. You could have called it "The Blue Room." Would you believe that I, who had never smoked, was put to bed for two whole weeks from passive inhalation? I was, yes, it's true, and the camp doctor told me I'd have to spend as much time as possible out in the open air to prevent its happening again.

My wonderful riding horse, which I had rented from Sammy Gay, who lived with his lovely wife across the street, helped me get away from it all, and I increased my riding time on the doctor's advice. I met Sammy through Mrs. Gay, one of the wonderful Australian ladies who cosseted our submariners. The Gays were fond of animals and they made every one of theirs a pet. One of their several horses, a pretty white filly, stood at the back porch every day with her front feet up on the porch floor until Mrs. Gay came out with a carrot or some other tidbit and patted the horse lovingly, and then and only then she would trot happily away. Sammy and Mrs. Gay had even got their big tomcat into an unusual and interesting habit. The cat, as all cats do, loved to catch mice. Whenever this one caught a mouse, he would stand at the back door and meow loudly until Mrs. Gay came out, looked at the mouse he had proudly brought to show her, and said, "You're a good cat." This was ample payment for his work, and he was pleased. He would then leave to work at catching more mice to show her. Mrs. Gay told us in the rec hall one day that she had hardly got a wink of sleep the night before because the cat began meowing shortly after she retired and, finally, at four in the morning, she gave up, got out of bed, opened the back door, and said, "You're a good cat."

One of those delightful pets was my beloved riding horse, Major, a gentle and talented riding and stock horse. He would sidle up to a gate and position me in the exact spot necessary to open or close the gate without ever having to dismount. On one occasion, he saved the day by helping me get rid of a stray steer which had wandered into the park and had eaten nearly all the flowers I had laboriously planted and cared for at the request of the Navy officer in command. No matter how I tried to get rid of the unwelcome guest, it eluded me at every turn, and people began standing around laughing at my exercise in futility. Finally, I ran across the street, mounted Major, and he made quick work of getting rid of the pesky intruder.

Major and I enjoyed many excursions through the countryside. We had one favorite ride several miles along the road running

Just a couple of pals. The author and her pet stock-and-riding horse, Major, R & R resort.

southeastward from our camp. The scenery was truly rural and pleasant. I especially enjoyed arriving at a gate built so close to the ground that it scraped along the surface, and it was entirely covered with wire mesh. It completely blocked the road. One had to open it, go through it, and then close it in order to reach the other side. It was a gate to a rabbit fence which was made up of wire netting extending up about three feet from the surface and, would you believe it, also extending about two and one-half below ground to prevent rabbits from burrowing under and infesting the area one wanted to protect. The Australians had given up on trying to clear the continent of this terrible pest, so they fenced themselves in, in order to keep the rabbits out.

Before very long, I had acquired a charming young friend, a contemporary. Her name was Grace Barron, a product of private schools, and herself a teacher. Like many Australians, she had a favorite riding horse, and we often went riding together. We took one memorable overnight horseback journey to see the northern part of the Darling Downs, the flatland in the area of the Darling River to the south and west of our camp. This flatland in the vicinity of the Darling is, as I have mentioned, the only land deep and fertile enough for farming, and it was devoted mainly to the raising of wheat. We saw only its northern edge. The outstanding feature of the whole journey was our overnight stay at one of the characteristic establishments of Australia, the rural hotel, located at a crossroads a day's travel by horse from the nearest habitation. Like all the other rural hotels, it was just a rather large house, family-owned and family-run, with complete and adequate service on a small, personal, homey scale. Charming!

While in Toowoomba, I was privileged to visit one of their public schools in which a reading class of about the fifth grade was in session. I was saddened to observe the physical facilities and the teaching methods, both of which needed modernizing. The reading instruction, in this particular instance, was entirely by rote, students and teacher reading aloud together in unison for the entire class period. The class was greatly overcrowded, too, with far too many pupils for any possible individual attention. Pupils sat on long benches; desk work was all but impossible, though a long shelf-desk stretched in front of each bench.

I was surprised to learn that in Australia at that time a young person who had finished the equivalent of the eighth grade was considered an adult and ready to join the work force as an unskilled laborer. Fortunately for them, technology was not as advanced and there were more opportunities for unskilled workers than was the case in most countries of Europe and North America. It was surprising to observe a corollary to this fact: there was no teenage society, only children and adults.

At the R & R, our dances were some of the best things we did for the men, and we owe a tremendous debt of gratitude to the many young ladies who came in large groups to be dancing partners. No young man had to sit out for want of a girl to dance with. Can you imagine what a treat it was to be actually dancing, yes, dancing with a girl, a real live girl, for a man who has spent months and months living in a cubicle with other men and always in mortal danger to boot? It was wonderful to see their happiness. As they were with us for only two weeks, there was no opportunity for the development of romantic liaisons such as were so much a part of the scene with the Marines at Camp Balcombe and Mount Martha. Thank goodness the young ladies also came in large numbers to socialize with the men on bingo and informal party nights.

I did make a discovery that surprised and shocked me, but which might not have surprised and shocked some other people. A dance had just started and I was standing near the door to greet volunteer girls who were still arriving when suddenly in strode an incongruous group of women, perhaps in their thirties, dressed in formal daytime street wear, complete with high-heeled pumps, fur jackets, hats, and gloves, and they walked in with an air of, "Step aside; we're taking over the place." I can see them yet. I brought Burdette over and asked him if he had any idea about who those people were. He very apparently did, for he politely asked me to go elsewhere while he took care of the situation, and he ushered them out. I asked him later who those strange woman were, and without hesitation he replied that they were prostitutes from a brothel planning on drumming up a clientele. Well, again I suppose it takes all kinds of people to make a world, and I began to think about what must have led the operators of that lovely downtown hotel to designate a floor for "Women Only." Regarding prostitution, I was not there to judge the men, I was there to help them, and who knows what we would have done had we been young men living in similar stressful conditions of mortal danger?

If one wanted to get important Red Cross business done it was necessary to travel the fifty miles to Brisbane, and I made the trip a few times while stationed in Toowoomba. In order to get there I would have to wait until some Navy person had official business there and ride in with him. The trip was an all-day affair, leaving me some leisure hours there after my errands were finished, and I got to know a little about the city.

On one trip I spent the extra time at the cinema, and this was where I learned, at last, the secret of a screw. The theater was empty and quiet, and I chose a seat. Soon a couple, the young man wearing an Australian Army uniform, took seats behind me, and he began to talk. "Got me screw to-dye [today]."

Guess what her answer was: "Ow lovely."

Then he went on, "Ten guineas, one pound, three shillings, and sixp'nce. Now we can get married."

At last! The mystery of the screw is solved! A screw isn't a screw at all. It's a paycheck!

Brisbane, pronounce "Brisb'n," was a pleasant medium-sized city built right at the place where the tropics begin. Many of its structures were built with an open strip at baseboard level and another opening where the walls join the ceiling, giving an upward movement of air which helped to cool the room. There were various other inventive arrangements for coping with the high temperatures, all interesting.

Besides an excellent and beautiful bay making up her harbor, Brisbane was endowed with another physical feature which was the envy of the rest of the continent: her huge, magnificent, flat, sandy Bondi Beach (pronounced "bon-dye"). Hundreds of people flocked to it every day all year to relax, swim, or play outdoor games.

Outdoor recreation was, and I am told still is, the favorite pastime of the Australian people. Swimming, tennis, and lawn bowling, which is called bowls, seemed to be the most popular, and those three pastimes appeared to be a way of life for them, along with the race meetings, excuse me, rice mee-tings, meaning horse races. Every city and town had a race course, which very often consisted of only a fenced-in plot of land with an improvised track. They held their race meetings every fortnight, with most of the townspeople attending and all placing bets, those that I knew of being very modest bets but still giving them the thrill of the wager. Not only were the Aussies devoted to horse racing, but everyone who could take care of a horse had one for riding, and they were used, too, in the serious business of sheep and cattle raising.

Outdoorsy and horsey, that just about sums up the Australian people.

Imagine my delight when word came that all of my beloved CBs who had earned R & R time were coming as a group to our resort. Quite a few of them had even postponed R & R so that we could all be together. As they wheeled into our yard, several whole busloads, they hung out of the windows and waved their jaunty white sailor caps and shouted, "Hi, Tillie! We're here, Tillie!" We had a wonderful time together and they entered into all our activities with gusto, as I knew they would. About halfway into their stay, one of them asked if he could tell me a secret; then he whispered that John Smith (obviously not his real name, although I remember it vividly) had hired a prostitute with the intention of spending the night with her. He had the bad luck of choosing one who was completely bald, and she, not wanting to let him know of it, waited until he was fast asleep, then removed her wig and laid it on the dresser. In the middle of the night, partially awakened, he reached toward her to give her a little gentle caress and patted, not her beautiful curls, but her bald head. He sprang out of bed and tore down the hall screaming for help because he thought he had lost mind and gone completely crazy. Poor guy, one of the horrors of war.

At the end of their R & R, such a precious and happy time for them and for me, my dear CBs boarded the buses which carried them away, and they hung out of the windows, again wildly waving their smart-looking white caps and shouting, "Good-bye, Tillie! So long, Tillie!" until their voices died away in the distance.

There is a terrible sequel to the CB story, too, and I received the information about a year later, surely by a true stroke of fate. Fate had moved my dear Red Cross friend Betty Thompson to invite me to visit her at her work at the Navy Hospital at the Navy Pier in Oakland, across the bay from where I was then working in an Army hospital in San Francisco. Betty didn't have any days off and she wanted to see me. I have told you a little about this visit earlier in this book and about the ward where Bill told me about his fall from the tree. Fate had led me to his ward, fate chose the day, and at the evening mess fate placed me at the only vacant set at a particular table. I know it was fate for there beside me sat the foreman of the work detail of the CB Chief Petty Officers' Mess back in Darwin. We could hardly contain our surprise at meeting again, and we launched into small talk about various members of the mess. He told me, for instance, about the best torpedo man in the entire Navy, who divided his time between Darwin and Perth. He had been a very busy man on those trips to Perth. He had impregnated six young women and they had all given birth in the same month. What a torpedo man!

My friend didn't talk, however, about the CBs as a whole, the whole battalion, and I finally asked about them. He averted his gaze and I thought for a moment that he must still be guarding some Darwin secret; then he was able to come out with it: "Where are they, you ask? In Heaven, I trust. They were strafed by Japanese planes as they debarked to start another assignment."

"All of them killed?" I asked.

"All of them killed, every one."

Oh, General Shepherd, where were you when I needed you the most! How could I have ever followed your advice and not let it get to me and simply say, "What a shame. Ping-Pong anyone?" I cried. And cried. And cried. And had to get up from the table and leave the mess hall.

Oh Japan, Japan! Why in God's name did you do this to us?

Personal relationships keep one's world revolving pleasantly on its axis, and I was blessed with many gestures of friendship extended by Toowoomba residents. Mrs. Yeates, whose son was a physician in Brisbane, invited me to her elegant home for afternoon tea and a visit from time to time. She asked me to bring along a friend, but my special friend, Jess Ireland, wouldn't go because Mrs. Yeates was a class above her. Oh, England, knock it off! What has class got to do with living? Aren't we all people together? I was another lady's guest, too, at elegant afternoon teas and garden walks. These were memorable treats for me.

An unusually interesting invitation was to breakfast one morning with a women's unit of the Australian Army. The menu was something I shall never forget: kippered herrings and canned—no, I mean tinned—baked beans. They were both good, too, and I was told that Princess Elizabeth, now Queen, enjoyed kippers as one of her favorite breakfast dishes. The servicewoman sitting next to me at this breakfast mentioned that she had just finished a tour of duty in, of all places, the Great Australian Desert. This was in August, at the depth of what passed for the Australian winter, and she told me something I had learned in geography class but had forgotten, that temperatures in the Great Australian Desert and the Sahara do not vary much from season to season, but they vary greatly between morning and night. The day before she left her post there, the noontime temperature had been ninety degrees in the shade, and the next morning they had had to break the ice which had formed in their washbasins.

My great and bosom friend was Jess Ireland. You can stand almost anything if you have a true friend. She had a husband and two boys, one seven and the other ten. She was one of the dear ladies who sewed for the fellows, mothered them, made koalas for me to ship home for them, and took part in our bingo and informal party evenings. She was the sister of Mrs. Sammy Gay, who lived across the street in front of our camp, and Jess's own home was across the street on one side of our R & R resort. Day after day I would slip under the barbed-wire fence, cross the road, and arrive in her kitchen for a spot of afternoon tea and talk. It was a joy to be with her.

Jess was an excellent cook. She had a way with curries, often used as the third-day reincarnation of the Sunday roast, called a "joint." Remember, Sunday hot, Monday cold, and Tuesday cut up into bits and served in a gravy-type sauce over a mound of rice. A good cook could do a lot with these. She was great with other types of foods, too, and her sponges could compete with the best of them.

She was also skilled in other aspects of homemaking, accomplished in gardening, knitting, sewing, and other handcrafts. She was a loving and knowledgeable parent. She enjoyed an active social life of her own which included lawn bowling, bridge, and that other Australian pastime which I shall now relate to you.

One afternoon, Jess said, "Tillie, would you loik to go to a rice mee-ting with me? We 'ave them every fortnoight."

I replied, "Yes, I'd like that very much. I like rice and I make a good rice pudding, but I've never attended a rice meeting."

At this she nearly collapsed with laughter, and said, "Oh no, 'tis the 'osses, thy run, don't you know."

We did go out to a rice mee-ting, at the track, no, the oval, one of those minimal but still very workable rural race tracks, bet a few shillings, and had a good time.

Jess helped me figure out how to live as an Aussie, which meant, among other things, conducting all financial transactions in pounds, shillings, and pennies, called pence. It is the pound sterling system, a pound equaling about $4.81 in our money, at the time, and it went like this:

- Farthing = one-tenth of a penny. I never saw one. I think it was out of use.
- Half-penny, called hay-p'ny = about one cent for us.
- Penny (plural is called pence) = about two cents of our money.
- Two-penny, called tuppence or tupp'ny and pronounced "tuppnce" = about four cents, for us.
- Three-penny, called thripp'nce and thrip'ny = about seven cents to us.
- Six pence, called six p'nce = about a dime to us.
- Shilling = twelve pence, a little more than our quarter.
- Florin (half crown) = two and a half shillings, a little more than our half-dollar.
- Crown = five shillings.
- Ten shilling note = about $2.50 in our money.
- The pound note = $5.00 in our money, exactly $4.81 at that time.
- The five-pound note = $25.00
- The ten-pound note = $50.00
- The guinea = one pound and one shilling.
- Twelve pence = one shilling, and twenty shillings equal one pound.

Imagine a seven-, eight-, nine-, or ten-year-old struggling to master basic math in the pound sterling system! Still, Britain had used it for hundreds of years, and every Australian had wrestled with it from

133

birth. But then, who are we to boast? All cookbooks were written in the metric system, and we're still struggling along with the teaspoon, tablespoon, cup, pint, and quart.

Jess occasionally became pensive, and one afternoon she mused, " 'Ow Oi'd love to go 'ome!"

I said, "Jess, you are home. You're sitting right here in your own kitchen!"

"Oh no," she sighed. "England."

Jess's husband was a hardworking, kindly man. She was devoted to him and called him "pet." For instance, "Ow's the toime going, pet?," which means "what time is it, dear?" Years later when talking about Australia with my husband, I told him that many Australian women called their husbands or sweethearts "pet" and asked him if he'd like me to call him "pet." He said if I did, he'd leave home.

Jess often spoke of Australia's need to modernize and urged me to visit a town about twenty miles away and see the way they (mis)handled their sewage problem. At her urging I went, and was I surprised! There was a narrow, shallow, V-shaped, open wooden trench along every street at the curb, and in the trench there slowly, very slowly, flowed, just trickled along, a tiny stream of open water. The little trenches and the water were not the surprising thing. The surprising thing was what floated along in the water: human feces and bits of crinkled rice paper, which passed for Australia's toilet paper, with flies galore lighting on their joyous find and buzzing away to visit the homes and the bodies of the citizenry.

Jess yearned over and over for the "mod cons" [modern conveniences], electric refrigerators, flush toilets, and hot and cold running water. She told me what toilets were like in Toowoomba and throughout much of Australia: because the soil was thin and the underlying bed of rock was very close to the surface, it was impossible to excavate in order to form a pit for catching the droppings, so the outdoor privies used by most home owners had a door in the rear through which the sanitary man placed a large metal vat, replacing it from time to time with an empty one. That was the role of the all-important sanitary man.

I asked Jess how the people up there in Queensland celebrated Christmas. She told me they did it the same as everybody else in Australia, with an elaborate feast centering around a magnificent roast turkey, a gala bottle of soft drink at every place, and the feast was followed by outdoor games. They couldn't have retired to the living room, for the majority of the homes in Toowoomba and climatically similar areas had only the large living-kitchen room, bedrooms, and the tiniest living room you ever saw, virtually a cubicle, furnished with a few chairs carefully chosen for their small size and dominated by the principal feature of the room, a fireplace to be used in case of great necessity in what passed for their winter season. So, even at Christmas, the postbanquet celebrating had to be either in the kitchen or by playing outdoor games. Anyway, outdoor recreation was the Australian way of life so it all fit perfect.

Jess told me then about the Christmas when they had had to do without the center of attraction of the whole Christmas celebration, the roast turkey. They had scrimped and saved to get the money together to buy the bird, and they finally bought and brought home the largest, finest one they had ever had. It was a live bird, and the question was where to keep it until the next day, when they would prepare it for roasting. There were no garages, no outbuildings except the privy, so they decided to keep it in the outhouse overnight. The next morning came, they went to the privy to get it, and—no turkey! Instead, there was a note which read: "How can I thank you for the marvelous Christmas present? No one has ever given me such a wonderful Christmas gift. If there is ever any special service I can give you, be sure to call on me. Your grateful Sanitary Man."

I kept in touch with Jess, more or less, and, a few years ago she told me in a telephone conversation that Newton Park had become a tourist park, which it was, in a way, when we ran it as an American R & R resort. Jess's husband had passed away and her two boys were on their own. Jess had continued her bridge, her bowls, and her rice meetings and had married a widower named Mr. Robertson. She had moved into his house and was enjoying her new life. Her new husband was not only a kind, good man, but he also had all the mod cons!

After I had been in Toowoomba seven months, a notice came that I had served my three years. I was eligible for home leave and was to terminate my R & R duty in two weeks. I received the news with mixed feelings, for I really didn't want to leave Toowoomba, the submarine crews, Burdette, the dear women, and the many, many young ladies constantly volunteering to dance and keep friendly company with the men. I didn't want to leave my magnificent stock-and-saddle horse, Major, and, most of all, I didn't want to leave my bosom friend, Jess.

And yet, I had gradually become homesick. The tension of three years of always being a stranger in a strange land, always on the move, and never being able to put down roots, had begun to wear on me. All that time, I had been so very transient that every morning my first thought on awakening was, *Now, let's see. Where am I?* and often I would have to cast my gaze around, go to the window, and look out to see some identifying feature and then say to myself, *Oh, yes. Now I know. I'm in Mornington,* (or Sydney, Adelaide River, Darwin, Brisbane, or Toowoomba) and oh yes, Australia, then dress and go to work. Strange, but it's an unsettling feeling, and I often thought myself to be in the same boat as the stiffly sedate English Army officer in Darwin who had sobbed on my shoulder, "Lily of the Valley! It reminds me of home!"

Leave-taking was marked by a surprise farewell party given by the dear volunteer ladies and friends, who presented me with a lovely five-inch-tall Waterford crystal vase, and I was quick-thinking enough to reciprocate with a brand-new copy of the culinary bible, *The Joy of Cooking,* which I had fortuitously tucked into my luggage on leaving the States. One young lady gave me the ultimate in charming small tea cozies, yellow, hand-knit, and double-layered, beautiful with colored yarn flowers nodding from the top. Back at home I bought a very small teapot so that I could serve afternoon tea with it. Another young lady gave me a pin in the shape of a widened version of the British royal crown, from an Australian warrant officer's cap. She had had it dipped in gold to wear as a lapel pin, a true treasure. I caught my breath on being presented with another gift. One of the ladies had been perpetually crocheting beautifully intricate lace around the edges of linen handkerchiefs, always and always working for months on end, her crochet hook never resting. We all admired them as she finished each one. Imagine my astonishment when she gave them all to me! That has to be love, doesn't it? The staff, too, gave me a farewell gift of six beautiful, very English cake forks, similar to very small dinner forks but with the first two tines bonded together to form one wide one. The chief cook, senior and top-ranking staff member, personally presented these forks to me, and he took even this occasion to remind me that, nothing personal, you understand, but he disapproved of women in, or connected to, the military. Still, the forks were lovely and the gift well meant, and who could not be grateful?

The farewell to my wonderful partner, Burdette Harrison, took place as we stood at the fireplace wall which contained the plaques of all of the submarine crews who had vacationed with us, filling the entire upper fireplace wall to the ceiling, with space left for only three more plaques. And the R & R resort was slated to continue on after I left. Burdette named off every submarine, the *Perch,* the *Guavina,* and on and on, and we reminisced about the crew members of each submarine, whom we had gotten to know, appreciate, and, as far as their few weeks would allow us, love. I have read since that submariners' loss of life was so great that if you went out on three patrols you could expect to be sunk; almost certainly after five; and if you had survived seven patrols, you were sure to be depth-bombed into eternity on your next sortie. As Burdette named one after another, he said after each one, "And they're gone—sunk. What a pity." By the time he had pointed out all of them, there were only three left that had not been sunk, and they were out on patrol and sure to suffer the same fate as the others.

I had made a valiant effort, but at last I could hold on no longer, tears and racking sobs engulfed me. My God, what a price to have to pay for freedom!

As I awaited transportation to begin the journey home, I thought of Australia and all I was leaving. I thought also of all I was taking with me. I was leaving, not that I wanted to, Mornington and its peninsula, Melbourne and her beautiful gardens, Sydney with "our 'arbor and our brrridge," Darwin with Manly Beach and its wonderful tides, Brisbane and her magnificent Bondi Beach, Toowoomba and her stunning Overlook. I was also leaving, and relieved to do so, "bloody," "fuck," Adelaide River, the Never Never Land, the wet and the dry, Army rations, powdered eggs, field directors, and the host at the party who had called me a camp follower.

I could not take with me the wonderful, grateful Australian people who never could do enough for us, so I had to content myself with bringing with me the cherished memories of their many gestures of kindness and the outpourings of loving friendship they had given me.

The dialect? No, I wasn't taking it with me. It had already become a part of me, like an arm or a leg. I had become an Australian by osmosis. I was a dinky di Aussie, fair dinkum.

XII

Happy Boredom aboard a Homeward-Bound Troopship

The four-week voyage home was safe, smooth, physically challenging, and boring. Sixteen hundred servicemen and one hundred servicewomen were packed like upright sardines into the troopship *General Mann.* You could take a walk, yes, if you went only a few steps and were careful about it. We women were "accommodated" in sleeping quarters, not to be confused with staterooms, twenty women in each one, piled up in four-tier bunks. Guess which bunk was mine? The topmost one, of course. That was the way I got my exercise, climbing up and down that ladder. And what if you had to get up in the night? I'll spare you a description of the journey down to deck level and along the passageway to the "head." Suffice it to say that we soon learned not to swallow any liquid except our own saliva after three o'clock in the afternoon. Up to this time I had been fortunate indeed regarding arrangements for my personal toilette, seldom having to resort to what my women friends of the Air Transport Command in North Africa referred to as the PTA bath: Pussy, Teats, and Armpits. But here a girl was lucky to get to wash her hands.

The Pacific lived up to its name; it was smooth as glass, with no seasickness—that was one big plus! But the boredom, it was colossal. Packed in so tight you could hardly move, no activities whatsoever, and unspeakable food: perfect reasons for the admonition, "Bear any hardship, cope with every inconvenience, graciously, and don't complain."

I don't know how the men handled the situation, but we women did find a spot on deck where we could sit on the floor—no space-taking luxuries, like deck chairs. What did you expect? This was war! So we passed the time talking, and here is a most peculiar oddity: No matter how the conversation began or what interesting subject we started out with, the talk always reverted to food. An innocent observation like, "On our trip to New Orleans, we did this and this, and we happened to step into a certain restaurant," and we were off and running about food and recipes. Or, "My mother was so good to us. She would always comfort us, she made all our dresses, and she was a wonderful cook," and we were off again on food, food, food: favorite foods, most memorable meals, embarrassing cooking boo-boos, spectacular holiday menus, and recipes, recipes, recipes.

Thus, the voyage progressed. Yes, it was incredibly boring, and yes, it was an exercise in coping with cramped, crowded conditions with nothing to occupy our time, but no one minded. We were going home, weren't we, and that was all that mattered.

On landing, I stood and watched as hundreds of men knelt and kissed the ground, and who could blame them? I would have, too, but my skirt was short and too tight to risk it.

XIII

Holding Hands with the Sick in San Francisco

I spent my vacation recuperating from surgery and immediately reported back to duty. The war was winding down and nobody was being sent overseas, but would I be willing to be a hospital recreation worker in San Francisco? Yes, certainly. Anything to help.

I was to be a recreation worker on the many, many wards of the enormous Army evacuation hospital named Letterman General Hospital, on the Presidio, in the Mission District. Sick and wounded servicepeople were brought there for treatment designed to bring their health back up to a stable condition before sending them on to specialty hospitals for plastic surgery or the fitting of artificial arms or legs, long-term treatment of chronic physical or psychiatric conditions—any special need. The hospital consisted of a multitude of long one-story wards of wooden construction sprawled over a sizable area. To the rear of the hospital grounds stretched an expanse of the Presidio land, sloping very gently upward as the eye traveled farther and farther into the distance, with patches of beautiful blue Scotch heather in winter and spring. One's heart leaped up on viewing it.

We had a Red Cross staff of about a dozen recreation workers and the same number of social workers, all stretched to their limit to meet the needs of this enormous hospital with nearly every bed occupied.

Two most insightful and important pieces of knowledge came to me in an in-service instruction session the first week of my duty: the role of recreation in the treatment of the sick and the difference between empathy and sympathy.

Recreation for the sick, anything that captures their attention and pleasantly focuses the thoughts on the activity going on, raises the threshold of pain and hastens recovery, and a positive attitude is a proven aid to regaining health. In other words, the pain has to be greater in order to feel it, and a happy mind leads to a healthy body. Many people think recreation programs for the ill are frivolous and a waste of effort, time, and money. This attitude, however, is not valid, although I know a CEO director of a huge veterans' hospital who, as of this day, thinks it is.

Sympathy and empathy are the same thing, only different. Sympathy expresses itself in loving, thoughtful kindness to one in trouble and getting a feel for what the sufferer is going through. The point is: it gets into your own emotions and you suffer with the hapless ill person. Empathy does all the same things that sympathy does, but the caregiver does not let the victim's suffering get into his or her own psyche, his or her own emotions, and one is able to walk away from the day's work physically exhausted, perhaps, but emotionally untouched, undrained, and able to tackle the next day's, the next week's, the next year's tasks with constantly renewed energy. However, if the caregiver allows his or her concern for the sufferer to get into his own emotional fabric, the stress will be unbearable, making it impossible to bear up for the long haul, the worker having to leave and go into some less stressful type of work. Sounds just like general Shepherd of the Marine Corps. His advice on how to take war was: "You can't let news of losses get to you, or you won't be able to continue, for you yourself will become a casualty and unable to continue with your work. You have to be able to say, and mean it, 'What a shame. Ping-Pong anyone?' " His advice had been a godsend to me and in spite of momentary overwhelming sadness on hearing of the total loss of the whole two Marine regiments, the whole CB battalion and virtually all of the submarine crews that had been guests at our R & R, I had been able to bounce back and carry on. This hospital admonition of empathy but not sympathy was also an enormous help and an absolute necessity, for there was immense need for tender loving care and consideration, coupled with the absolute necessity of being able, again, to carry on.

I saw some terrible suffering in those couple of years at Letterman. I saw a man who had been in a coma for six months. I also saw a big, burly man lying naked with no covers over him, half of his face shot away, one arm gone completely and the other severed above the elbow, and both legs off at the hip. The severed areas were raw and red, the man uttering only unintelligible syllables.

I worked for several weeks in a ward filled with rescued survivors of Japanese prison camps in the Philippines. Too weak to walk or even sit up, they were skeletons with skin on them, with bloated abdomens looking like the last stages of pregnancy of a woman with triplets, and sunken, staring eyes. And these men had already spent two months in another way-station evacuation hospital, building strength to survive the journey to Letterman. I could go on and on, but these three scenes remain so vivid that I see them as clearly and as shockingly now as the day I first gasped at the sight of them.

Recreation on the wards sometimes included just talking with various patients, often writing letters to their dictation, or sometimes running errands for them. However, most of this was done by wonderful volunteer Red Cross Grey Ladies, named not for their hair but for the color of their uniforms. This freed us for procuring and escorting volunteer musicians through several wards during an afternoon or evening, with violinists and vocalists usually the most appropriate because they were usually soothing and low-key. Though this was the most common type of activity, we also found other volunteers who contributed a variety of pleasant diversions.

Talk about following channels! That hospital took the cake. We had to ask, and then receive, permission from nine different people before we could bring any single activity to any ward, even for a few minutes. These included the head of our Red Cross Recreation Department, the doctor on the ward, the nurse on the ward, the chaplain, and five others. It's a wonder a person was able to bring in any entertainment whatever with all those regulations. I chafed under them—a gross understatement. Still, we managed to get the job done and I can't say enough in gratitude to the many wonderful volunteers who gave so generously of their time and talents.

The first year I was there, from Thanksgiving to the end of January, I never took off my raincoat, for I spent all my working hours delivering Christmas packages to hundreds of individual patients on the many, many wards scattered about the premises. That was recreation of the very best kind for them, those presents from home, even though, for me it was definitely not, because it rained every day all those two months.

One of the best things I did was organize and run a fishing club for ambulatory patients. It was highly popular and we had between a hundred fifty and two hundred members all the time. I rented large excursion boats and the men, in their dark red pajama-type hospital garb, piled into them for a day of complete happiness. We usually cruised to Carquinez Strait; the fishing was good there, and we always came back with a good catch, which was served up in their mess. The men were tremendously delighted with the club's activities. I even found a volunteer who taught them fly tying.

I often took ambulatory patients on other pleasant excursions as well: to the theater, to the park, to a garden party at a private home, and the like, and the community was generous.

We had our meals in the Officers' Mess, and it was there that I met the man who, three years later, became my husband. He was the Chief Finance Officer, a combat veteran of both World Wars I and II.

Life in San Francisco was a constant struggle with finances. Living expenses were so high and Red Cross salaries so low that young recreation workers who had just begun Red Cross employment had to write home for supplementary money to make ends meet.

I lived in a one-room apartment which had been a dining room in a private home on the far end of Arguello Boulevard, near Seal Rocks, and I could hear the seals barking from my open window. The apartment included a kitchen, dining alcove, bathroom, and bed/sitting room, all crammed into a converted standard dining room. You can imagine the small scale of those little cubicles! A fat person could never have squeezed into them. The only furniture the bed/sitting room could accommodate was a tiny table, a small straight chair, and a cot called a daybed, so narrow that all night you had to be careful not to move much or you'd land on the floor.

I went to work by streetcar, and, speaking of the quirks of war, here's one for the books: One day I was running a little late and just missed my usual streetcar and had to wait for the next one. As I entered the second streetcar someone called out, "Hello, Lill," a nickname no one but my family ever used, and there sat, on the front bench seat facing the door, my brother-in-law, Clinton Niles. He was an electronics expert, had joined the Navy, was stationed in Bremerton, Washington, and was in San Francisco on a one-day mission to install some electronic equipment in a submarine. We talked a few minutes until I had to get off at my transfer corner; we said good-bye and went our separate ways.

Everybody can remember where they were and what they did on V-E Day, May 8, 1945. On V-E Day, crowds poured into the streets of downtown San Francisco cheering and congratulating each other and, especially, the many of us jubilant people in uniform, ecstatic over the ending of the war in the European theater. We embraced each other, walked hand in hand, and the impromptu celebration went on far into the evening hours. I saw one serviceman climb up into a fountain and sit on its rim singing, with the water cascading over him.

V-J Day was, for me, something quite different, but equally, and probably even more, touchingly memorable. I was on duty in the Army hospital and had been assigned to spend several hours on a big ward filled with semiambulatory wounded men and had planned some appropriate celebration activities to mark, at long last, the surrender of Japan. One of the men, however, said he thought this was a day for reverent thankfulness. No use kneeling; these men were among the fortunate, brought back badly wounded but still breathing, at least alive, having seen their comrades killed all around them. He led us in a prayer which I am sure none of us will ever forget. We poured out our entire beings in the most heartfelt reverence, sorrow, and gratitude to the souls of the thousands and thousands of heroic servicepeople killed in the mass sacrifice which had brought us V-J Day.

On a brief visit back home to see a sick relative, I ran across two interesting sidelights on the war. (I'm sure you, too, have anecdotes of your own or ones told you by friends or relatives. Why not collect them into booklets for personal treasures and/or contributions to historical societies?) I sat one evening at the symphony beside a man who told me he had been head of a U.S. Navy supply depot, especially its finance department, in Nouméa, the capital city of the rather large island of New Caledonia. He told me he thought, as I did, that the United States was poised and virtually ready to invade the Japanese home islands almost immediately following the liberation of Iwo Jima and Okinawa. His unit had already received $10 million in

Japanese yen paper money with the words: "United States Invasion Money" printed on each bill. They had come packed in wooden boxes, each one labeled: "Toy Horse."

The other war sidelight came in a brief visit to a Milwaukee couple who were very close friends of mine, Dr. and Mrs. John Douglas. Florence, the wife, owned an antiques store, and John was a Doctor of Electrical Engineering at Milwaukee's Marquette University. In the course of the conversation, he remarked that he had invented sonar, a device which does in the water what radar does in the air: spot and indicate the location of objects, sonar indicating the location of waterbound vessels such as submarines and radar for spotting objects in the air. He had given his invention to the U.S. government as his contribution to the war effort.

We Red Cross personnel worked well together. We enjoyed each other's company, developed friendships, and socialized with each other. We were also entertained occasionally by various groups of loyal and generous San Franciscans. One such invitation came from the San Francisco Opera Company, which invited us to attend the dress rehearsal of the opera *Boris Gudonov.*

Boris Gudonov has never been one of my favorite operas. It brought to the stage one of the most curious episodes in the history of Russia, in the late fifteen and early sixteen hundreds. Boris Gudonov, brother-in-law and chief minister to the Czar, has caused the young half brother of the Czar and heir to the throne to be assassinated. On the death of the Czar, Boris, who committed this crime for the sole object of seizing power, ascends the throne. But about the same time a young monk escapes from his monastery, discards his habit, and goes to Poland, where he poses as the dead Czarevich. The Poles receive him cordially, feeling that it could be to their advantage to do so. He marries the daughter of a nobleman, puts himself at the head of the Polish Army, and marches with it against Russia. Just then, he hears of the death of Boris and in turn usurps power. Other events come to pass, but this opera stops there and it is well that it does, at least for us in the San Francisco audience, for we had spent the evening trying to surmise what it was all about. Each portion was seemingly unrelated to the one which had come before or the one which followed, with no dramatic progression toward a climax, and we at last realized that to understand the opera at all it would have been necessary to read, re-read, and re-re-read the libretto again and again to keep from getting lost in the monotonous maze of rumors, rambling reminiscences, and an unexpected scene in Poland. All this struggle to find and understand a story line could have been abandoned and we could have lost ourselves in the melodies had there been melodies to get lost in. We began to wonder why we had come at all, for the evening had been a total waste.

Well, not exactly, for suddenly the evening turned into a once-in-a-lifetime, unforgettable experience. The curtain opened on what must have been the last act, and our San Francisco audience was electrified. Not only did they see the pretender's troops milling around menacingly, but the San Francisco Opera Company had decided to put some strong dramatic punch into the opera after all by including a handsome white horse galloping fiercely toward the stunned onlookers who at first feared that the horse was galloping right into their very midst. They were noticeably relieved to realize that the horse was on a treadmill.

So far so good, but suddenly the situation took a highly dramatic and unexpected turn. The poor horse had to relieve himself, and a gust of air sent the excrement flying in bits and pieces up, up, and all around the stage. It stopped the show. Cast and audience alike burst into riotous laughter. A long pause followed, and all was silent. Then the entire audience rose as one person and gave a standing ovation to the horse!

How many people have been fortunate enough to be honored guests of a renowned opera company, to its premier performance, in graphic realism, of the gutter classic *That's When the Shit Hit the Fan!* This story could be titled: "All's Well that Ends Well," or "Ships That Pass in the Night."

People coming to San Francisco are told that no visit there is complete without an excursion to Pasadena's Huntington Art Museum to view Gainsborough's masterpiece *The Blue Boy* and its companion painting *Pinkie,* a full length portrait of a lovely teen-age girl, clad in an exquisitely beautiful pink silk party gown.

Following this sage advice, one Saturday evening after my workday and my dinner, I boarded the evening southbound train and ensconced myself in a vacant seat to enjoy the journey. Just as I became settled in my seat, I was joined by a Navy midshipman, older and more mature than the post-adolescent inductees one usually associates with Navy duty. He was in his middle to late twenties, affable, a pleasant seatmate. Service people gravitate to each other, and we made a well-accustomed sight, he in his blue middy and I in my Red Cross uniform.

We conversed pleasantly, sharing our service experience, and he showed me his wallet picture of his charmingly beautiful young wife.

As we neared Pasadena, his mood shifted to one of serious concern. "I can't let you go on a trek alone to find a hotel room. I'll walk along with you until we find you a hotel room and then I'll go on to the Navy base." I was grateful for his kind concern and we left the train together at Pasadena.

Knowing the city, he brought me first to Pasadena's largest and best hotel. Saying I wished to book an overnight room for myself, we were surprised at the desk clerk's blithe and tart turn down: "No rooms available," followed by a mock-sympathetic "SORRR-eee."

This scenario was followed virtually word for word at hotel after hotel throughout all of Pasadena as we walked through the streets of the city until near midnight.

Clearly we were left with only two options: Number one, to lie asleep on the sidewalk, and number two, to take drastic measures. We decided on drastic measures.

I went into the ladies' room of this last hotel in Pasadena, removed my uniform, and slipped into a dress which I had surprisingly and most fortuitously tucked into my overnight case as I was leaving my little apartment in San Francisco.

We then started our trek all over again, beginning at my first turn-down, the largest and best hotel in the city, and we asked for a room for two for the night. A broad, welcoming smile lighted the face of the night clerk who had so heartlessly turned me down a couple of hours before.

By this time it was past midnight with no possibility of public transportation to his Navy base, so my new friend had to face the prospect of spending the night with me. Puzzled about the one double bed, he wondered aloud, "Now how are we going to handle this?"

I answered, "I have an idea. I'll tell it to you, and then you let me know what you think of it. I know you are true to that lovely wife whose picture you carry in your wallet, and I have a gentleman friend, and besides, I don't indulge in sex escapades. You lie on this edge of the bed facing the outside, and I'll lie on the other edge of the bed, facing the wall. Once we hit the mattress there is to be no communication whatever, no touching, not even speaking a word. What do you think of it?"

He answered, "Let's try it."

We slept like logs. The next morning we breakfasted in the hotel coffeeshop. I thanked him profusely for his great kindness to me, we shook hands and went our separate ways. We never saw or heard from each other again.

One thing, though, I'm willing to bet: I'm willing to bet he never told his wife the strange story of the strange night he spent in the strange bed with the strange women in the strange hotel in the strange city named Pasadena.

During those two years in San Francisco, I never heard one negative comment about the internment of the one hundred ten thousand Japanese immigrants and their children—Nisei, sometimes referred to as Isei—after the Japanese attack on Pearl Harbor. To present-day historians and others, including the members of Congress and the White House, who in 1988 apologized for this "breach of civil liberties" and paid $20,000 to each surviving internee, I can only quote a slang phrase popular at the time: "Vas you dere, Sharley?" because such a reaction is typical if viewed from a peacetime perspective of no national danger. But the internment and relocation of Japanese and Nisei Isei was a measure deemed absolutely necessary in a time of national mortal danger and apprehension lest a fifth column of saboteurs and collaborators be at work within our own borders. Among one hundred ten thousand, how could there not be one posing such a threat? To investigate each one was obviously impossible, and time was of the essence. After all, our country, Hawaii, had been attacked and four thousand of its people, all U.S. citizens, killed, and the Japanese then had immediately seized our islands of Wake, Guam, and the Philippines. West Coast congressmen urged in Washington that the West Coast be evacuated and a defense line set up at the Rocky Mountains. As the war progressed, the Japanese did attack our mainland; they dropped aerial incendiary bombs on our forests of the Pacific Northwest, setting forest fires. They took, and occupied, two of Alaska's Aleutian Islands, Kiska and Attu. And they manufactured thirty-two-inch-diameter hydrogen incendiary (including napalm) bombs, floating them into the air from (supposedly) Mount Fuji, to be carried onto our continent by the winds of the jet stream. About four hundred of them are known to have landed in Alaska and on our mainland as far east as Michigan, one killing four people in Oregon, many being discovered years after the war ended.

So I ask you, were the Japanese a threat inside or outside of our country? I know the Nisei Isei suffered grave inconvenience, to say the least, but what else could have been done in the circumstances? The $20,000 granted each survivor makes sense, I'm sure, but in war you have to do what you have to do.

As I had been gone five years, and with the war over and much of its aftermath worked out, the notice I had been expecting arrived. I was to report back to my teaching post by Easter, 1947, or lose my tenure and my pension rights. In war, everything—yes, everything is temporary.

XIV

Just As Though Nothing Had Ever Happened

Back teaching in Milwaukee again, everything was the same: same school, same classrooms, same students only with different names, just as though nothing had ever happened. That was then; this is now.

Well, not exactly. I walked around as one under a heavy burden. My characteristic exuberant, sunny personality was gone. People said, "Tillie, your light's gone out."

I answered, "Your light would go out, too, if you'd been through what I have."

Our English Department chairman remarked one noon in the cafeteria, on hearing of a calamity, that calamity is the exception and calm peacefulness is the rule. I replied, "No, Frances. Calamity is the rule, and calm peacefulness is the exception."

I had also lost my interest in stylish dressing. A former student stopped me on the campus of the University of Wisconsin—Milwaukee, where I was enrolled in some graduate courses during the summer. She gave me a real tongue-lashing, a tremendous scolding. "You used to be such a classy dresser. We loved you and wanted to be just like you. Now look at you! You've turned into a middle-aged matron—nothing but a dowdy frump. Whatever's gotten into you?"

I replied, "When I was away doing war work, I saw so much suffering that now clothes don't mean much to me anymore."

She replied, "Well, if you don't care about looking stylish for yourself, do it for us. We can't bear to lose you." She was right.

The Able-Bodied Rec had become an able-bodied wreck.

Gradually, slowly over a span of several years, I got back my zest for life, my joie de vivre.

I never could understand, though, how men who I knew had been through far greater horrors than I had could calmly walk away from it all and return to civilian life just as though nothing had ever happened. Maybe they, like me, still carry it all deep inside themselves.

And now, here it is, fifty years later, and when I think of the thousands of valiant men with whom I lived and worked, heroes all, killed, almost all of them murderously slaughtered by the Japanese, I cry.

I still cry.

Historical Reference:
A Brief Account of the War in the Pacific

To the reader who wants to gain at least a bare skeletal historical ladder on which to hang the factual information making up these true stories, I offer this minimal account, read it if you wish. I also offer it to those of us who wish to gain a knowledge and understanding of those fateful events.

It is best to refer to a map of the Pacific Ocean, as you read it.

What Caused the War with Japan?

First, what brought on such a catastrophe? Japan is made up mainly of four home islands; an area about the size of our state of Idaho, with no natural resources, including no oil or coal, or iron ore, limited farmland, and, at that time, a population of about 80 million. The basic diet was fish, which they got from the Pacific Ocean, and rice, much of which had to be imported. The economy was, and still is, based on importing raw materials, manufacturing them, and exporting the finished products to the world markets.

Japan's Emperor traditionally reigns but does not rule. Through some power grabs by individuals, the government, lacking sufficient checks and balances, became dominated by the military, of which the Army was the more powerful. Thus, the Army governed Japan, and set the country on a course of aggressive territorial expansion southward, with the entire Japanese population believing all its massive propaganda.

Japan had already wrested Korea, Formosa, and Manchuria from China, amalgamating these acquisitions for several years, and now, taking advantage of China's governmental instability, had set about conquering and occupying China, province by province, governing with unbelievably horrendous atrocities such as mass execution of tens of thousands of civilians and POWs at trivial motivation. She had also deliberately sunk the American gunboat *Panay* in the Yangtze River. Then, too, Japan signed a military alliance with Germany and Italy in September 1940, toward the beginning of World War II.

These last three developments greatly distressed the American people, and President Franklin Roosevelt protested and urged business firms to limit their trade with Japan. This had no effect on the Japanese Army, the governing body, which then seized and occupied northern French Indochina. When she seized and occupied southern French Indochina as well, it became evident that she intended to use it as a springboard for conquering and occupying all of southeast Asia, the Netherland Indies, including Borneo, and even New Guinea, and amazingly, even India and Australia.

The United States reacted by calling on Japan to withdraw from French Indochina and China, but the Japanese, though they did not say so, had no intention of doing so, and our government froze all Japanese assets in the United States and discontinued all trade with Japan. Britain and the Netherlands followed suit, and Japan was bereft of her major trading partners.

There followed a long series of fruitless trade negotiations in Washington while the Japanese government (the military, dominated by the Army) quietly and industriously prepared for war.

When they felt they were ready for war, the Japanese government, which had not let its trade negotiators in Washington know anything about its plan, sent a telegram in code saying that November 29, 1941, was the deadline for trade negotiations and after that "something was automatically going to happen."

The code the Japanese used was broken by a skillful U.S. decrypter, and Secretary of State Cordell Hull announced the United States' terms for lifting the trade embargo and releasing the frozen Japanese assets: Japan's withdrawal from French Indochina and China and recognition of Chiang Kai-Shek as China's head of state, which the Japanese government (the military, dominated by the Army) was not willing to do.

It turned out that what was "automatically going to happen" was the Japanese surprise attack on the world's most heavily defended naval base, the U.S. Navy Base at Pearl Harbor, Hawaii, on Sunday December 7, 1941. The attack, almost entirely by air, lasted two hours, during which we lost over four thousand, two hundred lives.

Every ship berthed at Pearl Harbor was sunk. No Japanese lives were lost.

Although three aircraft carriers were out at sea and escaped destruction and all but one American ship, the *Arizona,* were later raised from the bottom of the ocean and repaired, our Pacific fleet was temporarily crippled.

The United States now had no choice. The next day President Roosevelt stated on a nationwide radio address that the United States was officially at war with Japan.

Japan's Immediate Aggressive Territorial Expansion Southward

Immediately after Pearl Harbor, the Japanese seized the U.S. island possessions of Wake and Guam in December 1941. They had seized the Gilbert Islands from New Zealand and had received a group of islands from Germany in appreciation for having signed a military alliance with Italy and Germany in September 1940.

Japan went on to conquer and occupy our Philippine Islands, all of southeast Asia, including about a third of China along its east coast, the British crown colony of Hong Kong, Burma, the Malay Peninsula, Singapore, Thailand, the Netherland Indies including Borneo (rich in oil), their prize island of Java, and also the northern portion of New Guinea. They bombed Darwin, Australia, on February 19, 1942, and even invaded eastern India. They did all of this by the first of May 1942, two months ahead of schedule, and all in four months' time!

America's Master Plan for the War in the Pacific

Gen. Douglas MacArthur had been the peacetime governor of the Philippine Islands. The Japanese invaded the virtually unprepared Philippines, with weak resistance, from December 10 through 24, 1941. On February 23, 1942 President Franklin Roosevelt ordered MacArthur to leave the Philippines. On March 12, 1942, he vowed, "I shall return," and boarded a PT boat with his wife and son, bound for Australia. They reached the vicinity of Darwin on March

17, during a Japanese air raid on Darwin's harbor. Maj. Gen. Jonathan Wainwright was left in charge of the Philippines, and he began surrender negotiations on May 5, 1942. The United States planned a two-pronged strategy for the war's Pacific theater. Gen. Douglas MacArthur was placed in command of the U.S. presence in Australia, which was to be used as our base of operations. He was also in command of military action emanating from there, close to the Asian continent, including New Guinea, Borneo, and the Philippines. Adm. Chester Nimitz of the U.S. Navy was placed in command of all military actions on the islands of the central Pacific Ocean, starting in the far south (with the exception of Guadalcanal, off the eastern tip of New Guinea, under MacArthur's command), and from there proceeding northward to include Iwo Jima and Okinawa, the two large islands closest to the home islands of Japan. MacArthur and Nimitz were to meet and join forces on Okinawa and use that island as their base for the invasion of Japan's home islands.

The Battle of the Java Sea

Their attempt to conquer and occupy southern New Guinea (the interior of this second largest island in the world is mountainous and an impassable jungle) by air and naval action led to the May 7, 1942, Battle of the Java Sea. It was fought off the eastern tip of New Guinea. It ended in a virtual draw with substantial losses on both sides, but it caused the Japanese to withdraw their landing troops and give up their plans to take the southern part of New Guinea.

Guadalcanal Begins America's War Strategy of Island Hopping

There followed a series of American thrusts to liberate or isolate Japanese-held island defense bastions, proceeding by planned logical steps northward preparatory to the invasion and conquering of the home islands of Japan.

This effort began at Guadalcanal, an island in the Solomons off the eastern tip of New Guinea, a difficult but successful six-month effort by the First Marine Division from August 7, 1942, to the end of February 1943. Other islands in the Solomon chain were also liberated by our forces; thus Japan was made unable to interdict American shipping to Australian ports.

The Bismarck Chain

Islands in the Bismarck chain followed, in a strategy of isolating a heavily fortified island by taking less important islands surrounding it. This was the beginning of the American policy of island hopping: isolating potential Japanese strongholds and bypassing them to strike where the enemy was weaker. This strategy was used to isolate the Bismarck Archipelago.

The Significance of Midway

On June 4, 1942, Japan attacked the island of Midway, part of the Hawaiian chain twelve hundred miles northwest of the Hawaiian island of Oahu, and an invaluable midway refueling base for either side's long-range bombers.

The one-day battle was a clear example of what naval warfare had become. No longer was the great battleship the queen of the sea. It had become only a protective screen for the all-important airplane carrier, with its flat top runway deck and its airplanes in their hangar below it and, most important of all, its highly skilled and experienced flyers. The Battle of Midway was fought only in the air, and Japan lost three of her four precious airplane carriers, as well as other vessels, 332 planes, and five thousand lives. The Americans lost one carrier and comparatively few planes and lives.

Japan lost heavily at Midway, seriously blunting their navy's striking power, and it was so decisive a loss that it turned the tide of the entire war. From then on, the war was not fought on Japan's terms, but on America's.

Japan Seizes and Later Withdraws from U.S. Alaskan Aleutian Islands

On June 6 and 7, 1942, Japan had attacked and occupied Attu and Kiska, two American Alaskan islands on the far western part of the Aleutian Island chain. The Japanese quietly withdrew from them after American submarine interruption of their supply line. They had taken the islands in a vain attempt to distract America from her intended attack on Midway, which they had hoped to take by surprise. At Midway, Japan had hoped to cripple the U.S. Navy but got her own crippled instead.

New Guinea Recaptured from the Japanese

The Australians, and American's other allies, worked at driving the Japanese out of northern New Guinea from mid-1942 to early August 1944. Australia had always considered this island, as previously mentioned the second largest of all the world's islands somewhat of an Australian colony, and its recapture from the Japanese protected the Australian continent from Japanese invasion.

Allied Strategy in the Pacific

All the Pacific fighting depended very heavily on air bombardments. The Japanese, who had lost about three thousand planes and far too many skilled aviators between November 1942 and December 1943, could not sustain losses at this rate, and so the Allies were able to establish air supremacy by midspring of 1944.

Australia was the base for the U.S. military operation against Japan. This operation was aided somewhat by whatever Australian troops were not already fighting in Europe or the China-Burma-India theater, and it was also aided, to a very small extent, by America's other allies.

America's great industrial strength, six times that of Japan and greater than the European nations of Germany, France, and Britain put together, made it possible to fight in both the European and Pacific theaters at the same time and mount a two-pronged Pacific plan of attack. One prong was up from New Guinea through the Philippines, the other skirting the center of the Japanese empire and advancing northward through the Marshall, Gilbert, and Mariana island chains to the island closest to the home islands. This was the island of Okinawa, closest to Japan, to be used as a base for a joint assault on the home islands of Japan. Japan had used the series of island groups as bastions for the defense of her new empire.

The Gilbert Islands Liberated

The first of the Navy's central Pacific island drives was in the Gilbert Islands, formerly a New Zealand possession, lying directly athwart the American supply route to Australia. The islands of Betio in Tarawa Atoll and Makin were designated as necessary to control the Gilbert Islands. The Makin attack began November 20, 1943, and the island was secured by twilight of November 23, 1943. Tarawa Atoll was difficult, surrounded by a coral reef and containing many underground caves. The invasion of Tarawa Atoll, the island of Betio in particular, began November 21, 1943, it was declared secure on November 23, 1943, though pockets of resistance remained for many days.

Taking the Marshall and Caroline Islands

In the Marshall Islands, only the Kwajalein and Eniwetok Atolls were to be taken, bypassing the numerous other Japanese strongholds in the chain. Kwajalein was a key Japanese communications center, a priority target. In January 1944, heavy aerial bombardment of the vicinity and the island began, followed by landings, and on February 7, 1944, Kwajalein Atoll was declared secured.

From February 17 to 21, 1944, the island of Truk in Eniwetok Atoll, with its important harbor and its usefulness as a Japanese staging area, was brought into American hands.

At the same time, U.S. Marines and the U.S. Army were taking Eniwetok, which was declared secure February 21, 1944, thus completing the capture of three main islands of the Eniwetok Atoll, opening the way for the American advance to the Mariana Island group.

Virtually all the Japanese defenders lost their lives in these actions. Had one deigned to allow himself to be taken prisoner, his family would have denied that he ever existed, it being a grave dishonor to surrender. "Save the last bullet for yourself" was the first line of written military instructions as a definite policy. Some, conquered unconscious, woke up in American hospital beds begging never to be identified.

At least one hundred ten thousand Japanese fighting men had been bypassed on the islands. Japanese aerial, naval and army strength had dwindled while American military strength had increased greatly.

The Mariana Islands' Liberation

Once the Marshall and Caroline Island chains were secured the next rung of the ladder leading to the Japanese home islands was the Mariana Island group, dominated by the three islands of Saipan, Tinian, and Guam.

Saipan had been slated for annexation to Japan and was the first contested island to have a Japanese civilian population. Twelve miles long, Tinian, a sister island to Saipan, was the site of a large Japanese air facility. From the runways of Tinian the Japanese bombers could venture as far south as Truk in the Eniwetok Atoll and as far north as Tokyo. The Americans wanted Saipan for it would place the Japanese home islands within the range of the new B-29 bombers. Guam had been an American possession since 1898 and had a native population of proud American citizens. Thus, it was both psychologically and politically important that Guam be liberated as soon as possible.

Saipan, twelve miles long, was considered the key to the Mariana Islands and is a hundred miles north of Guam. Honeycombed with caves, it was difficult to capture. Aerial bombardment began June 11, 1944, and on June 15, 1944, two Marine divisions and one Army division landed. It took them five days to get past the beachheads, and fighting was hand to hand from then on. The Japanese lost the island, at great cost in Japanese lives, and many civilians committed suicide rather than be governed by Americans, so effective had been the Japanese propaganda.

For the Guamanians, liberation was anxiously awaited. As the tide of the war turned, life under the Japanese had become a living hell, with various citizens executed for no apparent reason. An Army division landed immediately after the fall of Saipan on July 20, 1944, and after three weeks of fighting, with much strategic and physical support from the citizenry, the island of Guam was again free. Meanwhile, on July 24, the Mariana Island of Tinian was invaded and quickly liberated. Loss of life in all these island liberation drives had averaged one American to about ten Japanese. And now, after these losses of islands, the Japanese ruling elite at last realized that the war could not be won.

MacArthur Returns, and America Regains the Philippines

Gen. Douglas MacArthur had now been given the United States government's consent to begin his drive to liberate the Philippine Islands. But before his campaign could begin, the military planners deemed it necessary to secure the Palau Island group, a considerable distance directly east of the southern Philippine island of Mindanao, in order that MacArthur's flank be protected. The First Marine Division had orders to conquer Pelilu, a key island of the Palau group. They landed on September 15, 1944, to find the Japanese dug in extraordinarily well in underground bunkers and putting up unusually stiff resistance. The bloody struggle went on for nearly a month before the defenders were rooted out. A live documentary film of the invasion was made, titled *Fury in the Pacific.* Japan lost nine thousand, eight hundred of her ten thousand troops, killed, all but the two hundred who had been captured, wounded, or unconscious. The losses suffered by the Americans were horrendous considering the gains they made.

Some of the military, even including Admiral Nimitz, stated that this campaign may have been unnecessary, given American's great aerial superiority, which could have protected MacArthur's landings on the Philippines without it. At any rate, the stage was now set for the liberation of the Philippines.

The Japanese fully realized that a conquest of the Philippines would enable U.S. submarines to interdict what remained of their marine supply lines to their southern resource regions, such as Borneo and Java. Furthermore, far from welcoming the Japanese as liberators, the Philippine people viewed themselves as Hispanic-Americans. Aided greatly by American submarine activity from secret bases in Australia, the Filipinos developed an underground movement which grew to immense proportions and eventually played a very important part in the American liberation of the Philippines. This movement was at its strongest on the southernmost island, Mindanao.

It was decided that MacArthur's forces take the middle Philippine island, Leyte, first, and after heavy naval air bombardment, U.S. landings on Leyte began October 20, 1944.

A large Japanese naval force gathered at Leyte Gulf, where the Americans had landed on its beaches. The Japanese intention was to destroy the American supply train and, if possible, direct their fire on American troops ashore. At first the plan worked, but the next day the Japanese escaped after being confronted by a large group of American ships a short distance away from the gulf of Leyte. After damage to both sides' opposing ships, both sides retired. At the same time, another American carrier force met Japanese ships and destroyed four Japanese carriers and five other support vessels. Thus, all the remains of Japanese naval might was destroyed in the Battle of Leyte Gulf, and their navy would never recover. It had turned out to be the greatest naval battle in history, with massive Japanese losses. Oddly, the victory was partially the result of chance and a series of blunders.

The land battle for the island of Leyte lasted a full two months, with the Japanese surrendering ground only after inflicting heavy losses on the U.S. forces. By Christmas Day, 1944, the U.S. Army could declare the island secure, but "mopping up" continued well into the next year. The Japanese forces had been undermanned at the beginning, but forty-five thousand troops were poured into the attempt to stem the advance of the invading American forces. The loss of great numbers of these troops seriously depleted the numbers of Japanese soldiers available for their defense of the northern island, Luzon. By capturing Leyte, the Americans had cut the Japanese garrison on Mindanao, the southernmost island, off from their force on the northern island, Luzon, and the Americans could deal with the separate forces at their leisure.

MacArthur was now prepared to take from the Japanese the northernmost island, Luzon, with its capital city of Manila. With no chance of Japanese naval intervention, MacArthur scheduled his landing on Luzon on January 2, 1945, landing in the north and pushing the enemy southward and eastward.

On January 9, 1945, Lt. Gen. Walter Krueger landed parts of his Sixth Army at Lingayen Gulf, about halfway down the west coast, practically unopposed, and by January 29 had brought them into the vicinity of Clark Field, about a hundred miles or so to the south. In late January and early February, elements of General Eichelberger's Eighth Army made landings to the north and south of Manila, the capital, a little more than halfway down the island.

Though Manila had been declared an open city, that is, a city that would not be defended, it was pillaged and ravaged anyway, and the U.S. Army men took it block by block, beginning on February 3, 1945. The Japanese Marines committed unspeakable atrocities. They tied hospital patients to their beds and then poured gasoline on them and set them on fire, gouged out children's eyes, and raped and then killed women. On March 3, 1945, Manila was declared secure, but only after a month of bitter fighting. At least twenty thousand Japanese had died defending the city and its environs.

Corregidor was stubbornly defended as well, requiring a parachute drop on February 16 to help retake it. The fighting was bitter everywhere and military and civilian casualties appalling. MacArthur then used Manila as a port from which to pour in supplies for the remainder of the liberation of the island of Luzon.

The liberation of Luzon and especially Manila on March 3, 1945, marked the end of two and a half years of oppression for the Filipinos and also the end of captivity for a very large group of men who had been held in prison camps since early in the war. The Japanese code of Bushido does not allow for a soldier's captivity—he must, rather, kill himself—and the Japanese were surprised that Allied servicemen felt differently. Thus, they had no plans or arrangements for handling the prison population. The prisoners were subjected to severe overcrowding, malnutrition, lack of sanitation, tropical diseases, and brutal treatment. One in four died in captivity, and those who lived through the two and a half years of it emerged as ghostly wraiths with physical and mental infirmities that dogged them long afterward. By the end of 1942, the number of Americans held in Japanese prison camps was estimated at twenty thousand, most of them in the Philippines.

With the liberation of Luzon, MacArthur now took his men southward to recapture the southern island of Mindanao. The Philippine Archipelago is made up of some seven thousand islands, five thousand of them inhabited, and MacArthur stopped to liberate a few on his way southward.

The actions on Luzon had cost the Americans nearly eight thousand dead, and Japanese battle deaths are placed at one hundred ninety-two thousand. Thousands of civilians were also killed in the struggle.

The Americans landed on Mindanao on April 17, 1945. They were greatly aided by the inhabitants, who in some instances rose up and literally hacked the local Japanese garrisons of soldiers into pieces with bolo knives. About fifty thousand Japanese perished and perhaps twenty-five hundred Americans. POWs in prison camps were, mercifully, at long last, freed.

As previously mentioned, the guerilla movement, strong throughout the Philippines and strongest on the southern island of Mindanao, had been an amazing help in liberating the Philippines.

MacArthur went still further. He instigated a basically Australian reconquest of Borneo using the American Seventh Fleet and portions of the U.S. Army Air Corps under his command as well, allegedly to recapture oil-rich regions. Many say the Borneo action was not necessary.

MacArthur was now supreme commander of the Philippines, as well as all of the American troops based in Australia, and poised to fight as needed in all the Pacific military actions.

MacArthur has been criticized by historians for inept handling of many situations in his capacity as chief commanding officer governing the Philippines in the years it was an American territory. Also, they criticized him for being unaware that Japan would seize the Philippines immediately after destroying our installations at Pearl Harbor and therefore being unprepared. They also fault the MacArthur ego as a force to be reckoned with at every turn in the administration of the Philippine Territorial Government and in all consultations relating to the conduct of the war. However, they do credit him with having a fine mind, which, when he used it, brought about many good results as time went on.

The Japanese greatly regretted the loss of the Philippines. For Tokyo it was a staggering blow. Japan's critical supply routes to its southern resource regions ran astride the Philippines, and those were now completely severed by the American submarine effort against the Japanese Merchant Marine. The Philippines were the biggest logistical touchstone of the Japanese empire, and the Americans had conquered it. Life at home had in fact become a nightmare, thanks to the American effort against Japan.

The China-Burma-India Theater

During most of the war, the China-Burma-India theater, called CBI, was under a unified Allied command. It was little reported or publicized; the actual fighting in the CBI theater had little bearing in defeating Japan. The supply line to the CBI was the longest in the world, and compared with other areas of the struggle, it was constantly undersupplied. In spite of these drawbacks, it did have its own significance. It covered a vastly large area, and in general was heavily populated. The Japanese conquest and its political consequences gave rise to grassroots movements to rid themselves of their ruthless captors. Many of these groundswells developed into demands for self government. Ho Chi Minh in Vietnam was a prime example.

In China, the Manchu dynasty, which had ruled the country since 1911, ended when a republican revolution caused the Manchu emperor to abdicate. Dr. Sun Yat-Sen, considered the father of the revolution, led China from the Manchu abdication in 1911, until he died of cancer in 1925. His heir-apparent, Chiang Kai-Shek, became China's next leader, his regime constantly and seriously harried by three forces: the territorial aggression of the Japanese; Mao Tse-

Tung's drive toward communism, and Chiang's own inadequacies as a leader.

During the years 1894 to 1905, Japan had already wrested from China the territories of Manchuria, Korea, and Formosa. And now they had taken a large part of the Chinese mainland, mostly along the eastern part of the country.

The Communist party was a further threat to Chiang Kai-Shek. It originated in the south of China, but Mao Tse-Tung's "Long March" northward became an ever-increasing threat. As he marched toward the north, he campaigned heavily and drew large numbers of the mostly rural population to his brand of rural Communism.

Chiang needed large amounts of money to support his regime and he borrowed heavily from the United States. There was great danger of large amounts of this money being squandered, and to counter this threat, the U.S. sent Gen. Joseph Stilwell to China to be Chiang Kai-Shek's Chief of Staff of the Chinese Army in March of 1942. General Stilwell had had prior military service in China, he knew China well, and he spoke Chinese fluently. Although he was knowledgeable and efficient and did a great deal for China and her military, he had an Achilles heel; he was very sarcastic, earning himself the title "Vinegar Joe." Chiang strongly resented his sarcasm and kept requesting that he be replaced.

Another American prominent in China's war experience was Maj. Gen. Claire Chennault, a rather unconventional Army Corps general. He had come to China some years before the Japanese attack on Pearl Harbor to work with China's air force and Chiang appointed him chief of that branch of his military. In those years his crews were made up mainly of American flyers. In matters relating to aviation, he was a tactical genius. Previous to Chennault's tenure, the Italians had been in charge of China's air force and had left it poorly organized when they returned to Italy, even taking with them all the aerial maps of China. Chennault's airmen called themselves the "Flying Tigers." Chennault was a highly effective and skilled aviator and was a great believer in air power. In February of 1942, Chennault's expertise became all the more important when Japan occupied Burma. This permanently closed the portion of the Burma Road which ran from Lashio, in Burma, to Kunming, in China. This ended the only remaining supply route into China and supplies now had to be flown from northwestern India, eastern India being already in the hands of the conquering Japanese.

Because the Japanese had an air base at Myitkyina in northern Burma, supplies had to be flown over the eastern Himalayan Mountains, transporting them from India to Kunming in southern China, at an altitude of twenty-five thousand feet. This flight called "flying the Hump" was very dangerous, an aviator going down in those very high mountains could not be rescued. Stilwell and Chennault were constantly contentious with each other, Stilwell felt those supplies should go to the support of the Chinese army, while Chennault wanted the Chinese air force to get the support.

Stilwell did not engage in bribery but everyone else in the government did, so it seemed. Bribery was the basis of bureaucratic existence in China with its rampant, blatant corruption. Chiang Kai-Shek and his entire government were totally immersed in it.

In governmental matters, Stilwell and Chennault were in constant conflict. Stilwell spoke fluent Chinese and had a far better understanding of the army's military realities. Chennault, a tactical genius, constantly asserted that air power alone could defeat the Japanese. Chiang took sides with Chennault and kept insisting that Stilwell (and his sarcasm) be removed.

Chiang went to live in his chosen capital of Chunking and began gathering together supplies for fighting a war which he rightly predicted would come—a civil war with the Communists. He predicted that it would come the very day the Japanese surrendered to the American forces, and he was right. Although Stilwell regularly sent him military reports on the three-hundred division Chinese Army, Chiang was so lazy and incompetent that he didn't even know conditions within his own capital.

When the allied great powers held their conference in Cairo to decide on surrender plans for both the European and Pacific theaters of the war, Chiang's incompetence became clear to all participants, Stilwell speaking for him on all military matters.

Chiang had been receiving loans from the U.S. and continued demanding more and more. His bargaining chip was the argument that if China dropped out of the war, this would remove a million Japanese troops from China which could then be assigned to military action against the Americans. Using this bargaining chip, he received one and a half billion dollars from the U.S., and Chiang's blackmail was so great that about a billion of that went straight into his personal foreign bank accounts.

In October of 1944, Franklin Roosevelt finally bent to Chiang's pressure and had Stilwell replaced by Gen. Alfred Wedemeyer. Stilwell then led a Chinese army into Burma to fight against the Japanese, and continued farther south to work at creating a replacement for the Burma Road. The replacement of Stilwell, though, was a blow from which China did not recover, for Stilwell had brought the Chinese army to its peak and it never again attained that level of excellence.

The Japanese attacked southern China in May, 1944, to establish an overland route for the transportation of the rice crop of Indonesia to Japan. They also took some of Gen. Chennault's air fields but gained little from this.

Stilwell had predicted that Chiang's government would fall of its own weight, and this prediction came true. Chiang and his clique left and became exiles in 1949. How can a leader stay in power if he does not know his own people and is grossly disinterested in them?

The only Allied military successes in the China-Burma-India —CBI—theater occurred in Burma. Britain had lost Burma early in 1942, and was desperate to make progress in driving out the Japanese. Britain's loss of Burma had given the Japanese a border on India, the most highly prized colonial possession of the British Empire.

The Japanese consolidated their forces in India's neighboring Burma, with no objections from the Burmese. They knew that there was a groundswell movement toward independence in India, and they wishfully thought it might erupt in time to help their drive to conquer that great subcontinent. They waited for several months in Burma before launching their attack. India, though, aware of the possibility of a Japanese invasion, remained calm, and the Indian armed forces welcomed about two million Indian volunteers into the Indian branch of the British Empire's military forces.

Britain claimed that Burma would be again under British rule after the war, and to back up this claim she initiated a series of limited offenses against the Japanese in Burma. First they launched a series of nuisance raids called "Chindits." Next, Gen. Stilwell led a Chinese army group into Burma just south of its border with China. Stilwell's ultimate goal was to reopen the Burma Road, which had led from Rangoon, on Burma's south coast, up through Burma into China. The road had been the indispensable supply line into China. Stilwell was supplied by air. Meanwhile, work on a bypass of the Burma portion of the supply route had begun, coming up northward through eastern India, and then turning east at Ledo at the northeast corner of India, and then northeast above the northern tip of Burma and into China.

In 1944, an American infantry group calling themselves "Merrell's Marauders" inflicted some serious losses on the Japanese in Burma, but not as seriously as hoped for.

There followed another series of "Chindits," scattered attacks on the Japanese there in early March, 1944, which used gliders to land attackers behind Japanese lines, but this did not disrupt the Japanese attack on India, which had just begun.

Meanwhile, facing realities, the Japanese had reorganized their forces in Burma. As the war progressed, the Japanese could no longer completely supply all their forces in their conquered territories, and all had orders to make every military move a success with what they had, for Japan could not render them aid. The British, however, had recovered enough to make a very substantial commitment to the defense of India and the conquest of Burma on land, and the Japanese Navy no longer had ships available to make military maneuvers in the Indian Ocean. All in all, it looked as though the time had passed for the Japanese to consider expanding their empire, and yet, they invaded India.

The Japanese Burma Army was made up of about one hundred thousand men, divided into six divisions. Four divisions were in the northern part of Burma, and two in southwest Burma.

The Japanese began their invasion of India from central Burma on March 6, 1944. One division marched toward Imphal, just across the border, about two-thirds of the way south of India's northern border. Their aim was to conquer Imphal and by doing so, dominate the plain around Imphal-Kohima, which the British would use as a base for any move into central Burma; secondly to cut the railway into Assam, which passes through Maipur and carried many supplies into the portion of India just south of the eastern Himalayan Mountains. The British had expected the offensive but had no idea of its great size and they reinforced the fortress of Imphal only at the last moment. The Japanese began their siege of Imphal on April 4. It was defended by three British divisions. The British set up an air lift to Kohima and Imphal and began a relief campaign from India which reached Kohima on April 20.

The Japanese assaulted the heavily fortified English military base of Imphal with a stubbornness unusual even for their Imperial Army. The besieged garrison was aided by Americans running an airlift from India. However, the Japanese did not make any arrangements for aiding their forces, counting on using captured English supplies instead, so their troops began to suffer from malnutrition. Besides food shortages they were up against three drawbacks: they ran up against stiff resistance; the expected revolt against the English in India did not come to pass; and the monsoon rains began making the transporting of Japanese supplies virtually impossible. The siege of Imphal was broken on June 22, after 88 days, but the Japanese retreated relatively intact, and slowly, losing sixty-five thousand men, most from malnutrition, disease, and drowning. The British pursued them and caused them more losses.

The Japanese now reinforced and reorganized their army, bringing it up to two hundred fifty thousand men. They deliberately and very slowly gave ground to the British, allowing them to conquer portions of central Burma. Their thought was that their own supply lines would shorten, while the supply lines of their British and American enemies would lengthen.

The Japanese failed to realize the strength of Allied air power, not so much regarding combat air power, but logistically. All sorts of supplies were dropped to the British, a factor the Japanese had never dreamed of. Breakable supplies were dropped by parachute, unbreakables were free-dropped without parachutes.

By early 1945, four major Allied armies were busy conquering Burma: British troops were marching toward Okyab on the Bay of Bengal; a second British army was advancing on a broad front; a Chinese army was moving southward toward Burma on the north, and still another British army was marching toward the old Burma Road from the west. The Japanese resisted, but they intentionally allowed the enemy to march into central Burma. Merrell's Marauders made an attempt to push the Japanese against the British armies to be surrounded, but this attempt was unsuccessful.

The Japanese were thus forced to withdraw most of their surviving forces into Thailand. Here they were not welcome, for Thailand, like other countries which had tolerated, and sometimes actually welcomed their Japanese conquerors, had changed their minds about the Japanese and was mounting a drive for independence of her own. The Thais had mounted a resistance movement against their Japanese conquerors, conducting a brilliant campaign against the Japanese occupying forces in northern Thailand, aided by some native tribesmen who revolted behind Japanese lines. Thus, the Thais were able to make rapid gains against the weakened Japanese force, and by this time the Japanese forces in Burma had been reduced to little more than a nuisance.

The British extension to replace the Burmese portion of the Burma Road was finished by early spring of 1945, six months behind schedule. It had a pipeline running its entire length, greatly increasing its usefulness to China. It was called, at first, the Ledo Road, named for its northern Indian city where it turned east, but it was soon renamed the Stilwell Road.

The British realized by the spring of 1945 that they could take Rangoon, Burma's capital on its southern tip on the Indian Ocean and a major port, before the May monsoon rains began. A British amphibious landing was made on May 1, 1945, at the mouth of the Rangoon River, and on the same day the Japanese evacuated Rangoon, though the British landing force did not know it. The next day, a British aviator flying over the city of Rangoon discovered that the Japanese conquerors had gone.

By now the British had succeeded in overcoming an opposing Japanese army which was hardly their equal. The Japanese in Burma were feeling the crippling effects of the successful Allied submarine activity and were no longer capable of retaining the fighting ability they once had. As soon as the Imphal siege had been broken, the Japanese commanders were committed to a doomed withdrawal process. Their focus had been from enlarging their empire to simply maintaining their existing forces. The China-Burma-India action had shrunk into only side-line activity, having no bearing on the main war actions in the Pacific waters surrounding Japan's home islands.

After May, 1945, when the monsoon rains began, there was no more substantive action in Burma, the Japanese having been forced into a slow withdrawal into Thailand, an unpromising scenario because the Japanese Army in all of Malaysia was facing a strong and growing resistance movement.

India itself was the remaining part of the CBI theater. India had for years been plagued with civilian unrest; threat of religious civil war between Muslims and Hindus, and the country-wide resistance movement toward self-rule, independence from Britain. Self-rule did come, however, some years later, followed by the religious civil war some time after that.

The Japanese had controlled Indochina longer than they had any other of her southern resource areas. A rebel named Ho Chi Minh gathered guerrilla forces of Nationalists and Communists into a united group which liberated most of northern Indochina from the Japanese.

The war in the CBI theater was a matter of life and death to the men who fought there, but the Pacific war was neither won by the Allies nor lost by the Japanese in this theater of conflict, but despite its peripheral importance to the outcome of the conflict as a whole, it was of vast importance to the millions who inhabited those nations. The ruthless conquest and brutal governmental tactics of the Japanese in their aggressive drive of territorial expansion throughout southeast Asia served to sharply define and accelerate independence movements beneath, and some of them right on the surface. The Japanese conquest paved the way for the independent nations of southeast Asia that exist today.

Clearing the Way for the Invasion of the Home Islands

Iwo Jima is part of a small island group named the Volcano Islands. Eight miles square, Iwo Jima experiences frequent earth tremors and has no vegetation. It has steaming sulfur pits, abundant rock formations, and, on rare occasions, hot lava flows. The air reeks with sulfur. Almost seven hundred fifty miles south of the Japanese capital, it was part of Tokyo Prefecture itself.

The Allies would almost certainly have overlooked this island except for its strategic function. The Japanese had transformed it into a sophisticated observation platform, which included more than one radar installation. It functioned as their forward air raid warning station, warning of approaching American bombers from the Mariana Islands long before they reached Japan. In addition, the Japanese obviously intended to use it as a forward fighter base to interdict American air strikes against the home islands. If the island of Iwo Jima was conquered, the Americans could reverse this role and use Iwo Jima as a forward base for fighters to cover raids against Japan. Most important, an airstrip on the island, if of sufficient length, could be used to land crippled B-29 bombers returning from raids on the home islands of Japan. The Japanese decided to defend the high ground at either end of the island. Iwo Jima was dominated by Mount Surabachi. The volcanic ash, combined with cement, made extremely hard concrete. Working for months before the attack, they had honeycombed the island with bunkers, gun emplacements, and machine-gun nests, all well camouflaged. They also had three airfields from which the island could be contested. A garrison of twenty-two thousand Japanese defended it.

The U.S. Navy used six battleships to bombard this island for three days prior to the landing, but Iwo's fortification remained largely intact. At dawn on February 19, 1945, elements of the Third, Fourth, and Fifth Marine Corps Divisions, well over thirty thousand, landed on the beaches. Casualties were heavy from the very onset.

It took a full forty days to conquer the island, although on February 23 five brave Marines raised the American flag on Mount Surabachi in a scene immortalized in what became the most reproduced photograph of the war. American battle deaths were six thousand. The Japanese lost all their garrison except 212 taken prisoners. Thirty years afterward, geological expeditions to the island uncovered caves with Japanese bodies sealed in them.

The Marines wondered aloud whether it had been worth it. The Army Air Corps had no doubt. On the day the island was declared secure, March 16, 1945, sixteen B-29s returning from bombing the home island of Japan made emergency landings there. By the war's end, 2,252 other bombers did the same, saving the lives of 24,761 air crew. Iwo Jima became a small but vital cog in the American war effort against Japan.

Okinawa

This left one last island before Japan itself. Okinawa, the island in the Ruyukyu Chain that was needed as a staging area in an invasion of the home islands of Japan. Here was a direct preview of what the conquest of the home islands would be like. Okinawa was considered by many as being a fifth, if unofficial, home island, even though its inhabitants were culturally as much Chinese as Japanese. Japan had officially annexed Okinawa in 1879. Although the Okinawans considered themselves loyal Japanese, the Japanese did not arm the civilians on the island. Okinawa is sixty-seven miles long and from three to twenty miles wide, its average width is eight miles, and it has an annual rainfall of over one hundred twenty inches. It rains so hard one often cannot see his hands held in front of his face.

After the German Navy was essentially defeated, the British began shifting some ships to the Pacific theater, and for the first time in the island hopping campaign the Americans had some help from an ally, not relished at this point in the war, but accepted, and eventually proven helpful.

The Japanese commanding general prepared his one hundred thirty thousand soldiers, most of them Manchurians, to meet the Americans. They also conducted extensive propaganda among the nearly half-million inhabitants, telling them they would die if they fell into American hands and that the Americans had brought gorillas with them to tear civilians apart and other unbelievably gruesome lies.

On March 14, 1945, American and British ships began the isolation of Okinawa by bombing nearby islands, especially those that had airstrips or operational harbors.

For the first time kamikazes began their intended role on a large scale, with volunteer suicide pilots ramming their bombs into ships by air and by attacking in speedboats as well. The kamikaze proved Japan's most deadly weapon.

The attackers used two American Marine Divisions and two Army Divisions. No one knew Okinawa would be the last battle of the war, it was also the bloodiest.

On March 23, 1945, the Allied naval forces began the bombardment and aerial strafing of the island. On a nearby island, about three hundred fifty suicide boats were captured before they could receive their kamikaze crews. Each was to be operated by two or three men and was to carry something like an underwater bomb attached to a pole for bombing purposes, as well as hand grenades to pitch into American landing craft.

On the morning of April 1, 1945, Easter Sunday, the American task force reached the beaches of Okinawa. The Japanese had decided not to contest the beaches at the waterline. The Japanese garrison knew every topographical feature of the island. Japanese artillery fire would be coordinated, accurate, and deadly as never before, a fact evidently unknown to the attackers beforehand, who walked ashore with very little resistance. Some were ordered to turn northward, and they conquered the northern portion of the island with little resistance compared with what lay in wait farther south.

When the American troops turned south, they promptly encountered the Machinato Line, part of an interlocking system of fortifications that extended south almost to the very tip of the island. Artillery was skillfully hidden in cave mouths, making even sighting it almost impossible to the Americans.

The American forces, well over one hundred thousand strong, promptly engaged the Japanese in intense fighting, sometimes hand-to-hand. It was their worst trial of the war. Soldiers and Marines sometimes took temporary refuge in lyre-shaped burial vaults, especially during Japanese artillery bombardments. (Okinawans bury their dead above ground in concrete and stone tombs.) Flamethrowers were used on an unprecedented scale.

On April 6, 1945, a group of ten Japanese ships, led by the battleship *Yamamoto,* with their fuel tanks only 63 percent full—a definite suicide mission—left for Okinawa to destroy American landing craft and engage the American fleet. Warned by U.S. submarines of the mission, some carriers with their planes on the ready were sent from other U.S. island bases to meet them, and the suicide group was destroyed by aerial bombardment the next day. That was the last of Japan's naval forces—there was no more conventional Japanese naval strength left.

The kamikazes now began what was to be their greatest attempt of the war—to sink American warships. They flew in waves and destroyed thirty-one vessels. Thirty-five hundred kamikazes were destroyed by American guns on American gunships before they could slam into U.S. vessels with their suicide bombing. There was much wounding of American sailors in these attacks, mostly from burns.

The ground troops continued to experience trouble pushing south, but the problem was evidently now isolated and was most evident on their right flank. The Machinato Line of fortifications running down the spine of the island was pierced on April 4, although the Americans promptly encountered a second line, the Suri, two days later.

The Americans made a direct frontal assault, but now with a double development which would push forward on both flanks of the enemy's fortification line at the same time. The double development offensive was launched on May 11, and on May 31 both the Japanese right and left flanks were pierced, but with appalling losses to the attackers. On June 1, the final offensive to penetrate the Japanese fortification line on southern Okinawa began. The American General was killed by a bursting artillery shell on June 18. Four days later the Japanese General took his own life as enemy troops approached the cave in which he had his headquarters. A few days later the island was essentially secure, except that many Japanese survived in caves. Some emerged days, weeks, and even months later and fought individual battles, resisting to the end.

The casualties were the greatest that any single island had cost the American forces. About seven thousand, four hundred Americans died on land, and about five thousand more were killed offshore, mostly from kamikaze attacks on ships. About one hundred seven thousand Japanese were killed above ground outright, while an additional twenty thousand Japanese were sealed in caves to die of starvation, suffocation, or cremation if gasoline had been poured in after them and then set on fire. About four thousand Japanese planes were downed. The Americans lost 763 planes, 330 naval vessels needed repairs or were permanently out of action, and twenty-one ships were sunk.

Life for the civilians on Okinawa had been extraordinarily grim. They had not, to any appreciable extent, aided the Japanese military, although no small number took their own lives rather than be captured by the Americans, so heavily had they been propagandized. About seventy-five thousand civilians perished during the campaign. Many, however, were prevented from suicide by Americans of Japanese descent employed on Okinawa as translators equipped with bullhorns to advise the local population that death would not be their fate if they surrendered peaceably.

American physicians logged 14,077 cases of battle fatigue or neuropsychiatric casualties among the troops who had participated in conquering the island. Thus, the equivalent of a whole division had to be relieved, some, of course, for reasons other than wounds or physical illness.

Many servicemen questioned the value of the Okinawa effort, but immediately the Americans began readying the island for use as the home island invasion base and it became the receiving base for damaged bombers returning from raids on the home islands, saving thousands of lives and many American aircraft.

The Japanese Now Feel the Horrors of War Right on Their Own Home Islands, Leading to the Atom Bomb

The middle of the year 1944 saw the beginning of a highly effective use of a most remarkable airplane: the Superfortress, the B-29 bomber. It could fly farther faster and carry heavier loads than any other aircraft, able to carry as much as twenty thousand pounds. It had pressurized crew stations, making high-altitude flying comfortable, radar for ground mapping, and the gun turrets were remote-controlled. Gen. Henry "Hap" Arnold, commandant of the whole American Air Force, felt that it could bomb Japan into submission and shorten the war. After the Marianas were liberated in July 1944, they became the home base for the B-29s.

The campaign of B-29 bomber raids began in earnest on November 24, 1944, with a raid on a Tokyo aircraft factory. A hundred more raids were to follow, at five-day intervals. Weather and altitude combined to make precise target hits difficult, and in May of 1945 an experimental incendiary bombing at a lower altitude nearly demolished a large Japanese aircraft plant, and the practice of firebombing began in earnest. The bombing raids included as many as sixty B-29s at a time, all based on the Marianas. The bombs held napalm, which started fires immediately. At first targets were only industrial or war plants, especially airplane factories. Later, after the Philippines, Pearl Harbor, and the Bataan (Philippine) death marches, hideous memories for the American people, their aversion to attacks on civilians diminished, and a firebomb raid took place over a low-income section of Tokyo, causing fires that raged and devastated the area for four days. It was so successful militarily that Tokyo, Nagoya, Osaka, Kobe, and Kawasaki were all firebombed. Industrial areas, especially airplane factories, were always the best targets. The firebombing spread to middle-sized urban centers, also to isolated interior areas. Coastal areas were very heavily firebombed.

Fishing ships, furnishing the staple protein food, went to sea very little, and widespread hunger resulted. Though the aim of the bombing of the home islands was to hasten the end of the war, the Japanese refused to surrender. This would have been the ultimate degradation, unthinkable, death to be preferred instead. The people had believed all the propaganda that had been fed them. They believed they had been winning the war. They believed that American troops had been allowed to approach the home islands in order to make them more convenient targets for destruction by the invincible Japanese. Defeats had been routinely reported as victories, and now the Japanese people were told that the Americans could be expected to invade in order that they be mercilessly destroyed by a mass uprising of the citizens, 27 million of whom were furnished with spears of bamboo poles sharpened to a point at one end. Not only was fish scarce, but rice was, too, thanks to American submarines, sinking Japanese merchant shipping. And still the firebombing continued, right to the end of the war. Also, there was considerable aerial bombing of fortified key islands bypassed by liberating surrounding smaller islands around them, in the island hopping campaign of the American military.

The Japanese began making peace feelers that would be advantageous to Japan through neutral embassies: Switzerland, Sweden, Spain, always with the conditions amounting virtually to a simple cessation of hostilities, keeping territories, resuming trade, and all, especially keeping the Emperor, in whose celestial being was distilled the very heart, the essence of the Japanese soul. With these unrealistic expectations, they set the stage for the invasion of the home islands and prepared their people to expect it.

Thus it appeared that the next step would be invasion of the home islands themselves. MacArthur was to command the ground troops and Admiral Nimitz the landing of all troops, with appropriate air cover. The first troops were scheduled to land on the home island of Kyushu on November 1, 1945, and Honshu on March 1, 1946, with the plan of immediately taking the greater Tokyo and Yokohama area. There was great reluctance among the armed forces to invade, for it was expected to take a million Allied lives and many more Japanese.

The few who were privileged to know about the atom bomb began to think it might be wise to use it and thus avoid invading the home islands. Theoretical studies of nuclear fission had been going on during the 1930s, much of it by escaped German refugees who had fled from Hitler and his racist policies. Progress was slow on the bomb theory. Britain had a start on the bomb and offered it to the United States because that country could not afford its monetary expenditure and had no place safe from German air raids. The Manhattan Project to develop the bomb began in the fall of 1942, when the refugee scientists arrived in force and joined the American scientists in Los Alamos, New Mexico.

Germany had an atomic project in progress but later abandoned it. Japan did also but could not proceed with it because they lacked uranium. The American project went forward, however, because it was believed that an atomic bomb could make the Japanese surrender. The bomb was successfully tried out in the New Mexico desert on July 16, 1945. Its development had cost the United States two billion dollars.

President Harry Truman, who had assumed office some months before, at the death of President Franklin Roosevelt in May 1945, decided, after much agonized reflection, to use the bomb, and certain Japanese cities were ordered free of other aerial bombing in order that they might be used for testing the results of nuclear bombing. It was now widely believed by those who knew about the Manhattan Project that an atomic bomb would end the war.

The world entered a new age, then, on August 6, 1945, when a B-29, the *Enola Gay*, dropped the first atomic bomb in history on Hiroshima, virtually melting down the entire city, and three days later a plutonium device was exploded over Nagasaki.

Finally, at Last, Peace!

The Pacific war began and ended with the Emperor of Japan, Hirohito, but not in the ways one might think. To understand the war, especially its end, one must understand some unique and surprising characteristics of the emperor, his place in the government, and the decision makers around him.

As mentioned before, the Emperor traditionally reigns, but he does not rule. However, his influence is great. His role is that of a diplomat and ceremonial figurehead. However, he was, and is, still, the spiritual head of the state religion, Shintoism. Thus, he was an object of deep respect and virtual worship, many Japanese thinking of him as part God, part man.

The military in Japan had built itself into a position of inordinate power because the government was not constructed in a way to provide, as mentioned before, the necessary checks and balances. The Army acquired absolute power, became the runners of the government, by an extraordinary pair of power grabs by individuals. Prime Minister Tojo appointed himself Minister of the Army and then Chief of the Army General Staff. Thus, the Japanese Army became the undisputed ruler of the country. Any decision had to have the blessing of the Army. If the Emperor were to decide on a course of action for the country, the Army might decide he had been poorly advised and was free to disobey and substitute its own course of action. Anyone with a different opinion had to be most careful to keep secret his views, and particularly any action to advance his views, lest he be assassinated by the dreaded and powerful secret police, carrying out the Army's policies.

The Emperor had distinct reservations about the war from the very beginning. Even before Pearl Harbor he advised his ministers to adopt a national policy of moderation, a live-and-let-live policy. However, he was powerless in the face of the military, especially the Army. The fall of Singapore in February of 1942 convinced the Emperor that Japan could win the war, and in the spring of 1942 he announced that the war had been won.

Roosevelt's unconditional surrender proclamation on December 1, 1943, caused only a more stubborn determination by Tojo, who now additionally appointed himself, temporarily, Chief of the Army General Staff. The Army was the power in the nation.

After the Battle of Midway, when it became clear that Japan would lose the war, a Cabinet crisis developed. Tojo knew his power and influence had waned and he resigned, but the Army still determined stubbornly to fight on, though some ministers, clearly representing the Emperor, urged that the war be ended. It must be stated here that Tojo, Premier since just before the attack on Pearl Harbor, which started the war, was a relatively moderate government and Army leader. Others would almost certainly have been more extreme.

After Okinawa, Hirohito's closest and most trusted adviser told him that unconditional surrender was an inevitable necessity. Still the Army kept fighting on. Then, after Hiroshima, on August 6, 1945, and Nagasaki, on August 9, were bombed, unconditional surrender was all the more urgent.

This urgency was exacerbated by the Soviet Union's declaration of war against Japan and their military advance into Manchuria, as Stalin had promised the Allies that the Soviet would do three months after V-E Day, on August 9. It became a choice of did the Japanese want the Americans or the Soviet Union to occupy Japan? If the Soviets did, they would never leave and Japan's identity and her very culture would be destroyed, whereas the Americans would leave after their occupation of Japan.

Three of the ministers of the Big Six were in favor of unconditional surrender; three were for fighting off an invasion of the home islands. The Big Six was an advisory group of highly influential heads of government departments whose recommendations were usually passed virtually unanimously by the Diet, the national lawmaking body. The Big Six consisted of the Premier, the Foreign Minister, the Ministers of War and Navy, and Chiefs of the Army and Navy General Staffs. Because it was an unofficial body, its findings had to be ratified by the Cabinet. Since the Big Six was evenly divided on the matter of fight or surrender, they asked Emperor Hirohito to voice an opinion. He said, "I have given serious thought to this situation at home and abroad and determined that my people must suffer no longer." He realized that his subjects were willing to die for him, but he could not require such a sacrifice. The very survival of Japan as a nation was at stake. Immediate surrender was the only means to ensure that Japan would live on as a unified nation after the conflict. When the Emperor finished speaking, the decision had been made. In order for this decision to become national policy, it had to be approved by the Cabinet. The meeting of the Big Six had taken place very late on the night of August 9. The surrender policy was quickly approved by the entire Cabinet early the next morning, August 10, 1945, with the proviso that the monarch retain his throne; otherwise they would fight on to the bitter end. The American Secretary of State replied that "the ultimate form of government of Japan would be determined by the freely expressed will of the Japanese people."

There were deliberate attempts by individuals and groups to sabotage the surrender process. In spite of some delaying arguments among some Japanese leaders, Hirohito never doubted that his people would keep him on as Emperor, and on August 14, 1945, he prepared a recording of a surrender proclamation which was broadcast to the nation at noon the next day, August 15, 1945.

On August 27, 1945, General MacArthur entered Tokyo to take on his role as leader in charge of occupied Japan. On September 2, 1945, the official ceremony took place aboard the battleship *Missouri*. So strong was the Samurai mind-set of no surrender, no personal acceptance of being taken prisoner in battle, "save the last bullet for yourself," that Emperor Hirohito had to ask the Japanese representatives personally not to commit suicide lest the Allies get the impression that killing themselves would invalidate their signatures. General MacArthur and Admiral Nimitz signed the surrender document for the United States, and representatives of the other major Allies, now members of the United Nations, did also.

The cost of the war in the Pacific theater had been enormous. Japan had lost one and a half million battle deaths and well over 3 million civilian casualties in the air raids, including Hiroshima and Nagasaki. Total American casualties, killed and wounded, were later set at 296,148. Britain, Australia, and other Empire/Commonwealth countries lost 185,000 in battle deaths. At least 4 million Chinese had been killed. There were also untold monetary losses and personal suffering by those who lost their homes and families in the war and those who had been brutally treated by the Japanese.

It was very hard for those in the Japanese military, and for the Japanese people in general, to accept the idea of leading the life of a defeated people, since the ingrained, second-nature Samurai code demanded that in such circumstances the only honorable thing to do was commit suicide. In fact, many women, terrified of what the Anglo-Saxon conquerors might do to them, made sure they had on hand the poison capsules given out by the government during their preparations for resisting an invasion of the home islands. Perhaps the people expected the same atrocities their own soldiers committed against the conquered populations during their aggressive drive to conquer and take over the governments and the people of Southeast Asia, including the Netherland Indies, Australia, and India.

Mass suicide might have been the people's response to the surrender had the Emperor not admonished them that their lives were necessary for the rebuilding of Japan.

MacArthur bent his attention and energies to a makeover of the Japanese government into a pattern he thought suitable, but he neglected the needs of the general populace. Food rationing, in particular, was far too skimpy for basic sustenance and forced the people to patronize a thriving, greatly expanding black market in order to stay alive. Still, in general, the people were grateful to MacArthur for one all-important thing: he refused to permit the Emperor to be tried as a war criminal. Had MacArthur allowed it, there would have probably been a civil insurrection. Anyone knowing the complexities of the Japanese culture—and very few Americans did—would know that the Emperor, as the traditional head of the national religion, Shinto, was the very soul of Japan and, in a way, the very soul of every citizen. Also, anyone who understood Japan would have known that the Emperor was only a bystander in the Pacific war, was actually against the war, and, in fact, many of the military's aggressive expansionist drives were begun by the military rulers of the country without letting the Emperor know anything about them.

The people of Japan put their thought and energy into peacetime economic progress.

MacArthur was relieved of command in 1951. By that time the nation had made great strides forward, and the wars between the United States and the Communists in Korea and Vietnam primed the economic pump in Japan, leading to the staggering growth and development of the Japanese economy that is much in evidence today. Some say they have accomplished by peaceful means what they had tried and failed to do by force. Still, their economy remains in a very delicate balance. They still must import their raw materials, including all of their oil, coal, and iron ore. For this reason they could never survive a war, with its naval blockades and other countries adopting policies of export-import trade restrictions. The Japanese people have planned their economy on a very long-term basis. They have indeed followed the advice given in Emperor Hirohito's surrender speech: "Keep pace with the progress of the world."

Map of Australia

Map of Pacific Islands

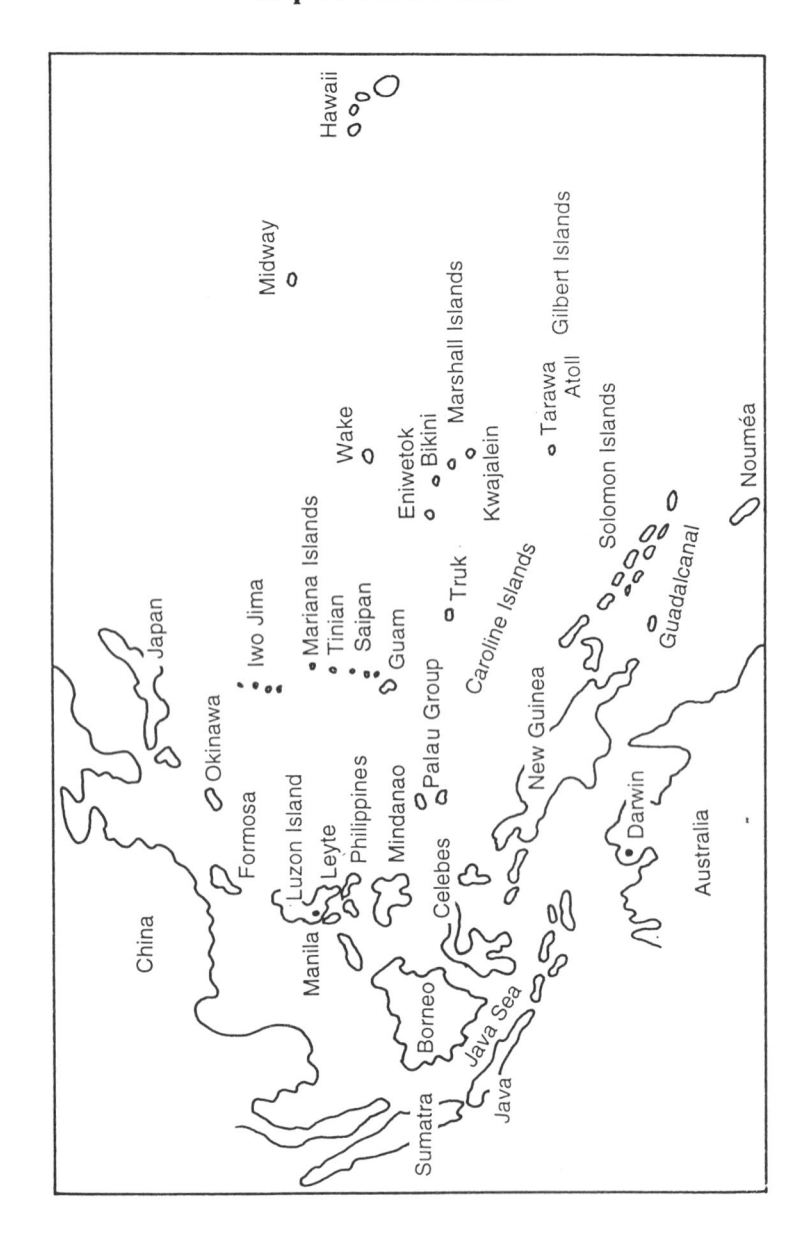